Happily Ever After

CB80

A Tribute to Marriage
by a
Fifty-Year Veteran

by

Del Hayes

**Happily Ever After: A Tribute to Marriage From a Fifty-Year Veteran
by Del Hayes**

Published by Homestead Press, 1690 Estates Parkway, Allen, TX 75002. 972-727-3693. First edition. Visit our website at www.homesteadpress.com for information on bulk orders.

ISBN-10 0-9822706-0-7
ISBN-13 978-0-9822706-0-8

Library of Congress Control Number: 2008943245

Printed in the United States of America.

Cover design and page layout by His & Hers Creative
www.hisandherscreative.com

Dedication

This book is dedicated to that pretty, blond nineteen-year-old girl who, on an April night in 1956, permitted me to take her to the Sophomore Class play. That night changed my life, and I will be forever grateful for that.

Contents

Acknowledgements

Obviously there would be no story without that pretty, nineteen-year-old blonde. Not only did my wife Colleen make this book possible, she offered many helpful suggestions and critiques as she read various drafts. There were also the occasional "Did you really intend to say THAT?" sorts of challenges that kept me on track.

Then, I have to thank my son, Clint, for all his valuable editing assistance. His experience as an editor was crucial in helping me convert a decent draft into a final manuscript, ready for publishing. He also prepared my book cover design.

I also appreciate the unnamed literary agent who, though rejecting an early query, took the time to write a brief observation that led to my changing the focus of the book, thereby greatly improving it. Dr. Stacy Ikard, the Associate Pastor at our church, was kind enough to take time from her over-full schedule and read the manuscript. She offered keen insight based on her years of experience as a minister, marriage counselor and college professor. I am grateful for all of that.

Finally, I want to thank my friends who read the drafts, and offered their insight as representative of the young couples to whom the book is addressed. Their comments helped me judge whether I had in any way accomplished my goal of holding up marriage as the best choice for our lives.

Thanks to all of you.

Del Hayes

Foreword

For decades I have stood in front of young couples on the most important day of their lives—their wedding day. For me, their parents and the congregation a poignant question hangs in the air: will they make it? Will they sustain this relationship and weather the years ahead? We hope and we pray for the best but ultimately, on that day, we recognize that their future happiness rests in Divine providence and in the way they accept and nurture the blessings of love they receive.

My friends, Del and Colleen, have done just that. Their story witnesses to a life-time of simple, yet important, decisions to respect, trust and honor one another. In doing so, they built a life to be admired and celebrated. Those of us who know them believe it a gift to be a part of their life. But in this book we have a more excellent gift—reflection upon their marriage for the sake of others.

Happily Ever After: A Tribute to Marriage From a Fifty-Year Veteran is a rare peek into the nooks and crannies of an honest, real, ordinary fifty-year marriage with extraordinary candor and insight. Del and Colleen's story rings with sweetness and devotion; a moving journey to be enjoyed. What they have to share with those of us who care about marriage makes their journey all the more special.

Marriage remains a precious gift from God—no matter what sort of mess we make of it. Del and Colleen remind us that with commitment, care and Divine help marriage can be the single most important blessing in life; "believing all things, hoping all things, and enduring all things," to quote the Apostle Paul.

When I close the traditional wedding service of worship, I speak the ancient biblical words, "May marriage be held in honor by all" (Hebrews 13:4). It is my hope and prayer that the couple standing before me will be blessed with a life-giving marriage, and that marriage as a life choice will be protected and nourished by all.

This is Del and Colleen's hope and prayer as well. These fifty-year veterans have much to teach to anyone willing to listen.

Dr. Stacy Ikard
Associate Pastor
Canyon Creek Presbyterian Church
Richardson, Texas

Introduction

On a snowy day in January 1957, I stood at the front of the Evangelical United Brethren Church in Iola, Kansas, and watched as Colleen Cady came up the aisle on the arm of her father, to join me and become my wife.

On a rainy day in January 2007, she and I stood together in a hotel near Dallas, Texas, welcoming friends and family who had come from far and near to join us in celebrating fifty years of that marriage. This book is about what those fifty years have taught us about marriage, and why we believe that the commitment to marriage is so important in our lives.

Over the years of my marriage, and as I worked on the manuscript for this book, I have had occasion to read a number of books on marriage. One of those was *Why Marriages Succeed or Fail*, by Dr. John Gottman, a marriage research scientist of many years standing. In the Preface of his book, he makes the following statement:

> This book is not about me, nor is it just another opinion about how to have a good marriage. My expertise is in the scientific observation of couples....The couples who have participated in my studies...have revealed the hidden natural laws of relationships.

I believe that Dr. Gottman and I share the same goal: to help couples have a successful marriage. But beyond that, I differ from Dr. Gottman in that this book is, in fact, about me—and my wife, Colleen. I suppose you could also say that it is "just another opinion" on the complicated subject of marriage.

Unlike Dr. Gottman, and the many other credentialed experts on marriage, I have no expertise in the scientific observation of couples, nor do I have a PhD in marriage counseling. What I do have is a rewarding, successful marriage of more than five decades, and I believe I have learned much about those "hidden natural laws" to which Dr. Gottman refers. I also believe I have learned much about what is required to have a lasting marriage. So I offer here not the voice of the expert, but the voice of the veteran, the voice of experience.

What I also have is a deep and abiding belief in the value and importance of marriage, and of its superiority over any other lifestyle choice that a couple might make for their lives. That this opinion is not shared by a growing number of couples is obvious to even the most casual observer of our society. It has been my nature to speak out on issues that trouble me. And the erosion of the importance of marriage to us as individuals, and to our society at large, troubles me. So I have chosen to speak out, through this book. It is a very personal statement of my beliefs about a very personal life choice.

I have for many years been a private pilot, and have occasionally subscribed to *Flying* magazine. A regular feature in that magazine is called ILAFFT (the editors jokingly refer to it as "I laughed"), which stands for "I Learned About Flying From That." Stories are submitted by readers, and describe experiences they have had while flying. Although sometimes humorous, because of dumb mistakes made by the pilot, the experiences were always educational. Hence, the name. The pilot learned some valuable lesson from his experience, whether humorous or life-threatening, that he wished to share so that other pilots could learn from it as well.

I could have, similarly, called this book "I Learned About Marriage From That." It's rather hard to make a catchy acronym out of that, so I left the title as it is. Nevertheless, the point is the same. The book is based on experiences Colleen and I have had during our fifty-plus years together, and what I learned about marriage from them.

Colleen has kept a diary since she was a freshman in high school. We thus have a record of every day of our lives together, from the first day we met. Those diaries were an invaluable source for writing this. They served as a reminder of our experiences together. Where it was relevant I have included excerpts from her diaries, as well as a few from my own journals. In each case, I have discussed in detail what I learned from those experiences. Some are humorous, some are embarrassing, others very rewarding. But all were educational.

I have read that when two corporations merge, such as when Exxon bought Mobil Oil, it can take years for the employees to all feel part of the new entity—and some never accept the change. In a very real sense, that same phenomenon occurs in a marriage. Two people, with disparate personalities and emotions, who have been accustomed to doing things their own way for all their adult lives, wake up some morning and find themselves merged into one legal entity. They suddenly are expected to do things, not the way they have always done it, but the way someone else has always done it. Conflict is virtually inevitable.

We each bring to a marriage a laundry basket full of our personality traits. Are we moody, or annoyingly chipper? Are we rational and logical, or prone to making flippant decisions based on our emotions of the moment? Are we a person of deep faith, or atheistic? Are we a morning person, or a night person? Every one of these traits, from the most trivial of how we hang our toilet paper to our deepest beliefs on life, are part of the deck of cards that is put into play in any marriage.

How that merger, that marriage, fares is entirely dependent on those two people, on their commitment to making it a success, and how they resolve the inevitable conflicts. That is determined by the two individual personalities, their beliefs, how they were raised. In short, the success of the marriage is dependent on the factors that led the two of them to decide to get married, what each expects from the marriage and is willing to put into it.

This book is about one such marriage—namely, my own. To understand what I have to say about marriage in the remainder of this book, I think it is necessary to know at least a little of who Colleen and I are, to know something of our personalities and our beliefs, how we were raised and what brought us together. How two people meet, fall in love and come to be married become the opening scenes in the drama that is their marriage, setting the stage for all that follows. Our personalities and beliefs influence our marriages, and our attitudes toward marriage, just as surely as the beliefs of the employees of Exxon and of Mobil Oil affected that merger.

I could have told you who and what Colleen and I are simply by listing our personality traits in terse clinical, psychological terms. That would have served the purpose, and would have been most expedient—but it would probably have been even less enjoyable to read than it would have been to write. Instead, I wrote it as a short story, a sort of novella, of how we met and came to be married. That story influenced our marriage for as long as we've been married. We still talk about various aspects of those few months between our first date and our wedding, and how they affected us.

As you read our story you will begin to perceive personality traits that would later affect our marriage. Perhaps you will see some of yourself in them. You will also see those traits reappear in some of the experiences I describe in later chapters, and see how they affected our marriage. That happens to most of us. We are often too immature and too infatuated with our new love at the time to be able to see the personality traits in each other that will come to influence our marriage. I talk about that in detail in a couple of later chapters.

After telling our story, I delve into some of the experiences that have caused me to be so concerned about the status of marriage in our society, and posit three answers to the question, "What's happened to marriage, today?" The rest of the book is devoted to what I believe to be the fundamental prerequisites to a good marriage, and why I believe so unconditionally in marriage as the best choice for our lives, and the best answer to most of life's problems.

It is my hope that by sharing our experiences others may benefit from them. It is far more personal than I would have been able to share in my earlier years. But the longer I am married the more I have come to believe in it, and the more concerned I have become by what I see happening to it. So I swallowed my inhibitions and started writing. My goal is to help other couples reach this same stage in their marriages, looking back over fifty years, and feel the same warm glow that Colleen and I now feel about ours.

Chapter 1

Sixteen Days

September 7, 1955

What a day! First day of college. Was mixed up all day. Couldn't find classes. Studied three hours tonight. Chemistry is going to be rough. Met lots of neat kids. Really missing David already. Hope he makes it down this weekend.

Poets would have called her farm home rustic. She had grown up knowing the hard work and privations that defined the life of farmers during the Depression. But those years are called the formative years for a reason. They had formed in her a strong sense of hard work, and dedication to whatever task was yours to be done. Rather than feeling deprived, she developed a pride in herself and confidence that she could not only overcome any obstacle, but could excel.

Colleen was a bright child, the kind of student that made the teacher of her one-room country school glad to be a teacher. And through her eight years of being nurtured by a caring teacher she came to love school, to love learning. But most of all, she developed a passion for excelling at her classes. To make less than the best grade, to be less than first in her class, became tantamount to failure. It was a passion that would guide her life.

She carried that passion with her when she left her country school and went into the nearby rural town to high school. As were so many country high schools of the time and locale, it was quite small. Colleen graduated Valedictorian in her class of seventeen. But high school had not been all studying. During her freshman year she met David, and they quickly became a couple.

They had a lot in common, and it soon became accepted by all that they would some day get married. And she wanted that. She wanted to marry and have children, to raise a family. As in everything else, she wanted to excel at marriage and raising a family. Her marriage would be her profession. And to excel at her chosen profession of home-making she believed she needed a college degree in home economics.

David planned on a career in coaching, and had received a scholarship to a four-year college. But a four-year college, and living away from home, was expensive. With no financial assistance, Colleen decided to attend the junior college at the nearby county seat. She could live with her aunt, who lived there. With a part time job, she believed she could manage. So shortly after her eighteenth birthday, she moved out of her lifetime home and moved in with her aunt to start college

It would be hard, they agreed, being separated. They had been together virtually every day for four years, and each counted on the other's presence. David had already moved to his faraway college. It wasn't all that far, but he had no car and little in the way of public transportation was available. Long distance telephone calls were an expensive luxury, so they would rarely get to talk to each other. He would come down to see her on weekends whenever he could find a ride, but they would have to depend on letters to help them stay close. It seemed they had left for separate worlds.

And for her, JuCo, as she came to know it, was a whole new world. She was eager to see what existed outside her cloistered small-town childhood. David would be her husband, but that would be after college. She felt they should each date a little, have some new experiences, before they settled down. David reluctantly concurred. It would help them be even more sure of themselves, she assured him.

Colleen believed in plans, and it was her plan to attend the two years at JuCo then finish her degree at the state teachers college. It had a strong home economics department, she had been told. But a home economics degree required fifteen credit hours of chemistry. Her small high school had not offered chemistry, so it was an unknown and she feared it. Still, it was required. She had never let difficulties keep her from her goals, so she would take chemistry and was determined to excel at it.

On that first day at JuCo she walked into the wood-frame chemistry building at the corner of the small campus, not knowing what to expect. It was to change her life forever. She had no way of knowing that, of course. She was apprehensive, inwardly fearful and intimidated. She had already learned that the chemistry teacher, Mr. Kennedy, had a reputation of being stern, demanding, his classes difficult.

The class was mostly guys. Several of them had taken high school chemistry under Mr. Kennedy. They had what appeared to her an insurmountable advantage. But no one knew how fearful, how intimidated she felt.

She had recognized in her diary, at the close of that first day, that chemistry was going to be rough. As the days went by, it got rougher. Her fears of chemistry weren't unfounded, but she did find help.

October 8, 1955

I don't know about this chemistry. I'm not sure I'm going to survive it. Ray S. and Rob N. came by to do problems and study for the midterm, tonight. We got quite a lot done, but I don't feel ready for the test. I'm so tired. I don't know if I can keep this up all year.

Over the weeks of struggling over problems and studying for exams, she and a few of her classmates had become close knit. They often came to her house to study. It's doubtful that any of the guys would have denied that they could have studied just as well with each other, somewhere else, but no one would have thought of excluding her. She had become part of the gang, and they liked her.

By mid-term she was beginning to establish herself as the equal to the guys. But it seemed easier for them, and she succeeded only by her determination to do so. She studied endlessly for every class, every exam. Each night she went to bed exhausted, sure that the next class would be her undoing.

February 7

I'm just lost, weighted down, up against a brick wall today. Mr. Kennedy just went outlandish in his assignments, and I just <u>can't</u> get it done. I've never felt so at my wit's end. I'd just give up if this keeps up and say to heck with college. Then I could marry my man—and make us both miserable.

As usual, she persevered. Still, JuCo wasn't all work. She had been selected to be a cheerleader for the basketball team and had been asked for dates by several guys. It was new, and exciting. But she missed David, and he missed her. He came to see her as often as possible. She was determined to see college through, and knew that getting married would ruin that for her. So she would wait, continuing to push herself to excel in her classes and enjoying the attention of an occasional date.

Rob, one of the chemistry class group, had begun asking her for dates. She liked him and had fun on the dates. She was young and naive, and did not recognize the signs of trouble to come. Rob was becoming seriously interested in her. But David was her guy, and she had no interest in a new relationship.

February 28, 1955

Well, here I am nearing the end of my first year of college, and I'm good at it! I'm so glad! The kids like me and so do the teachers. I was afraid I wouldn't be a success at it, but I'm all the way around. It's a swell feeling to know you can do it.

All in all, college was going well. She was gaining confidence and beginning to truly enjoy it, and had been asked to fill a vacancy on the Student Council. She continued to date Rob occasionally, but was beginning to recognize that he was far more serious than she wanted him to be.

March 17, 1955

Went to the library with Del 'til 3:00 today, then home to study.

It was the first time she mentioned him in her diary. She had noticed him almost immediately when chemistry class started. Like her, he came from a farm. He had attended the local high school, so knew lots of the students and had been elected president of the JuCo freshman class. He was easy to talk to, and helped her with the chemistry problems—especially the math, which was her nemesis. He was fun, and she enjoyed being around him.

He seemed to always find something to joke and laugh about, and didn't appear to take the course as seriously as she did. Still, he was one of Mr. Kennedy's high school students and had also been Valedictorian when he graduated. She considered him to be competition, but neither of them thought much about it in those terms.

She was curious about him. She often wondered if he would consider asking her for a date. But he was going steady, she had been told. So they would study together, enjoying each other's company, each wondering if the other might somehow be interested in them.

He had noticed her when she first appeared in his chemistry class. She seemed different from the local girls he knew. She was pretty, with short blond, wavy hair that he liked, and had bright, blue eyes that seemed to sparkle when she smiled—which she frequently did. There were other girls in JuCo who were pretty, but he was not particularly interested in them. They often seemed superficial. She had a nice figure, was trim and athletic looking. But other girls had good figures. That wasn't what he most noticed.

She was obviously smart, more than holding her own against the guys in Mr. Kennedy's class, and that impressed him. Of course, there were other smart girls in JuCo but they were generally withdrawn, bookish. He was friendly to them, which was his nature, but had no interest in them.

But she was different. There was an electricity about her. It was in her eyes, it radiated from her face. She exhibited an exuberance for life that shined in her eyes. She was young, excited about her new life, eager to savor every new experience and sip from the cup of coming of age. So when she entered a room, people noticed. And so had he.

He was chairman on the student council committee responsible for preparing decorations for the annual JuCo Spring Banquet. She had been appointed to the committee, so they were together a lot while working on it. They enjoyed each other, felt comfortable together. But he was going steady, and she was committed to David.

The months of separation were beginning to cause cracks in her relationship with David. She had urged him to date a little, and he was beginning to do so. Rob was very serious about her, as she was beginning to recognize. She tried to back away, telling him they should stop dating—but Rob wasn't willing to concede. Del and Rob would study together, and talk about her. So Del knew that she was not totally committed to David—or to Rob—and would wonder about her.

May 26, 1955

Darn! I miss school!—like fury. I'm lost without seeing all the chemistry kids—Del, Allen, Rob, and all the rest. I even miss Mr. Kennedy.

Her first college year had ended. It had been an exciting year of accomplishment, of growth and self-discovery. She got her A in chemistry both semesters. And stern Mr. Kennedy had become her friend, advising her and helping her to adjust to her new world. She needed just one more semester of chemistry to meet the requirement for her degree.

Mr. Kennedy was already beginning to suggest to her that if she took the full twenty hours she would have a minor in chemistry. She would then be able to get jobs in the chemistry department when she left for the state teachers college to finish her degree.

He even suggested that he would help her get a job with the big chemical firm located there. But that was too daunting for her to think about. Summer was starting. She would have to work, but wanted to relax and enjoy her free time.

She spent her summer days at work, and evenings swimming, going to movies and the band concerts in the park. Guys were home from various colleges, and she got to have several dates with them.

August 31, 1955

Tonight I realize my perfectly wonderful summer has drawn to an end, and I hate it so. I know I'll be tickled to death when school starts tomorrow, but tonight I'm all apprehension. I've sure changed this summer. I know David is still my guy, but somehow I can't seem to be satisfied with just him. I wonder why?

It had been her coming-of-age summer. She had her own money, and was feeling grown up and independent. She had some dates, causing her and David to have a serious falling out, but they patched it up. She felt they had been going together so long they needed to be married—but that was not a step she was willing to take while still in college. They agreed again that they loved each other enough to be able to wait. She turned her attention to the new semester, beginning her sophomore year— her last at junior college.

September 7, 1955

A disappointing day. I was nominated for Student Council elections, and I didn't make it. Had been nominated against Del for President.

September 15, 1955

Finally got a letter from David. He said he was sure we would break up when school started after the way I acted all summer. He's so wrong. Del and I had to hand out lab supplies for three periods today. Had lots of fun.

September 16, 1955

Elected Cheerleader! Really looking forward to it. David won't write me. Guess I've made him mad again. Del mentioned today he wished I was on Student Council. Me too.

Classes had started. But this year she knew the routine, was part of it all. She was disappointed about not winning the Student Council election, but Del had been the freshman class president and was much better known than she. The very fact that she had been nominated was recognition of her growing acceptance in JuCo and made her feel good. The gang was together again in chemistry. The class was even more difficult than the previous classes, but her confidence level had grown—and the guys were always there to help. Mr. Kennedy was even more supportive, assuring her that she was the equal of any of the guys. So she continued to work herself to exhaustion, determined to excel.

She and David had resolved their problems and she was already missing him, but her growing popularity at JuCo was exciting and she liked being asked for dates. David found that hard to handle.

September 27, 1955

Rob came over to study tonight. He surprised me—I thought he had gotten over me. Stupid guy. First thing I knew Del drove up. At it again. Rob said he thought Del was half way stuck on me. I hope not. He's got a swell gal. I just like to joke and cut up with him.

September 28 1955

Got put on a Student Council program committee today with Del and some others. Don't know why. Guess they just wanted me.

September 29, 1955

Messed up something awful in chem lab today. Nothing close to what I was supposed to get. Del came by tonight to help me fill out my lab manual. I don't know about him. We went to the library to get a book, and just visited. Then he insisted I go get a coke with him—and he's supposed to be going steady!

October 10, 1955

Did a good job at board in chem today. Del and Rob came by tonight to get problems. Stayed till 10:30. Del left last. He sure is fun. Too bad he has a steady.

October 13, 1955

Got chem lab procedure first try today! Skating party tonight. Wow! Del broke up with his girl last night, and wanted to bring me home. Sure I'd like to go with him, but what's the deal? I'm afraid I'll just be the "other woman," and I don't like the feelings that would cause one bit.

October 17, 1955

Del is still wearing his own ring. Maybe I'll get to go with him yet.

October 21, 1955

Went to game tonight. Saw Del there with his girl. Guess they made up.

October 23, 1955

Studied for while, then went to a movie. Del there. He brought me home after buying hamburgers. Don't know about that boy.

November 29, 1955

School holds no charm for me all of a sudden. I hope I get over it. I'd better! I'm about in the mood of preferring to get married, and that's out of the question.

November 30, 1955

Went to assembly this AM. They had a "mock marriage," with all guys. We about died laughing! Del never pays any attention to me anymore.

It had been a tumultuous, and pivotal, semester. She was learning new things about herself. Her life was inexorably heading down new, and unexpected, paths that she was only beginning to perceive.

Del had shown a real interest in her at the first of the semester, even temporarily breaking up with his girl. Del knew he was attracted to her, but she seemed to stay committed to David, and he couldn't seem to quite bring his relationship with his girl friend to a close. As winter closed in, a form of stalemate, or impasse, seemed to have set in.

Colleen's feelings about David constantly vacillated. When they were apart they would hurt each other's feelings, then he would come down to see her and all would be well again. She continued to believe that David and she would eventually marry. But that was always in the future, after she had her college degree.

The chemistry gang continued to study together. She would see Del and his girl friend at the games, or in the hallways, and assumed that he was still unavailable. He made no further attempts to get a date, and seemed to have stopped showing any interest in her. Rob continued to study with her, but made no overtures. She and David saw each other as often as he could get down. When they were together all the old feelings seemed to be real.

So Christmas came, as did the New Year, and the first semester of her last year came to a close. One more semester and she would graduate from JuCo. She would be leaving to attend the four-year teachers college, with little likelihood of ever seeing any of her friends from chemistry again. But she had bigger problems weighing on her.

December 8, 1955

Oh Lordy! Mr. Kennedy trying hard to get me to take Quan next semester. Should I? I don't think I can handle it. Del came by about 9:30 to work on lab manual.

December 13, 1955

Well, I guess I'll give up and take Quan. Mr. Kennedy had a long heart to heart with me about how I would need it.

She had without question become Mr. Kennedy's favorite student. He liked her dedication and effort, and did all possible to guide her into the field of chemistry. She had come to love him as a teacher and a friend, and respected his judgment. He assured her that she could handle it. Besides, all her chemistry gang would be there. They would continue to support each other. And Del had told her that he was going to take it.

January 18, 1956

Got a call from the chemical company today. They said to come on down to interview. Mr. Kennedy gave them a letter of recommendation for me. I guess he likes me as much as I like him—and that's a lot!

By convincing her to take the full twenty hour program, Mr. Kennedy had been able to get her lined up for employment with the large chemical company while she finished her degree. Her future was veering in a direction totally unimagined by her when she started college. The last chemistry course was much harder than she had feared. Even though everyone helped her, she knew she was in over her head. But, as she had always done, she refused to give in and studied even harder than ever.

And Del had let her down. He had decided at the last minute that with ten hours of high school chemistry, and fifteen of college, he would be better off for his engineering degree to take more math. So they saw little of each other as the last term crept to a close. Winter slid into early spring, and her life seemed to consist of either being in the chemistry building, or studying chemistry. Her relationship with David stayed rocky, as it had before. David was upset that she was going to move even farther away, to work for the chemical company for the summer.

March 14, 1956

Rob came by to study last night. We had coffee—was very cozy. The attention I'm getting from Rob again keeps me from missing David. What kind of a person am I?

March 15, 1956

Our first performance of the play. Went off better than practices. For some reason Rob and Del have regained interest in me.

March 16, 1956

Last night of play. Went even better than before. Spent whole noon hour visiting with Del. Then he asked me for a date for Saturday night! But I didn't accept because I was afraid David would come down. Sure do want to go with him.

March 17, 1956

Spent whole day at work fussing at myself for turning down Del's date. But David did come down. We spent the whole time fussing about me being gone for the summer—as usual.

Del could no longer ignore his interest in Colleen. He didn't get to see her much in class, so started dropping by to visit her at lunchtime at the chemistry building. They would sit on the steps and visit. He always felt comfortable with her, liked her company.

April 6, 1956

Been moping all day at school. Can't quite believe it's true that David and I are really breaking up, after six years. I've thought of it, but never believed it would happen. Has it? Band concert tonight. Sat next to Del. Upset his girlfriend. Guess I can't blame her. He's sure nice.

April 10, 1956

Whee!! David isn't mad at me, but doesn't want to make up.

Rob came by to study, then asked me for a date "since I'm free now." Then Del came by on a shaky excuse to "work on the class prophecy."

April 12, 1956

Spent whole darn day at chem. lab. Del came by and sat on steps visiting with me during lunch.

It was becoming plain to Del that he could no longer resist keeping company with Colleen, however he had to do it. As Student Council president, he was responsible for all the planning and preparations for the annual graduation banquet. He was also responsible for writing the Class Prophecy and a reminiscence about the previous two years. He had arranged to get Colleen appointed to the banquet committee. They would be spending a lot of time together.

Two years of separation had taken its toll with David. Her dating bothered him, in spite of their agreement. He also could not see why she had to go to the state teacher's college, instead of coming up to finish her last two years at his college so they could be together. She kept telling him that it did not have a good home economics department. But she secretly feared they would not be able to resist getting married. She didn't believe she could handle marriage and college, and was determined to finish her degree. So he had finally called it quits—although neither one could quite believe it was going to stay final.

April 15, 1956

Del came by to work on banquet stuff, and spent all Sunday afternoon. Stretched out on couch and read jokes to me while I tried to work. Asked me for date tonight, but Rob had already asked to take me to movie. I've got trouble. Rob is really serious. I shouldn't have gone out with him. Told him nothing had really changed with David. I didn't mean to hurt him. I'm such a fool.

April 16, 1956

Back to chemistry all day. I'm so tired tonight I can hardly stay awake. Am looking forward to my date with Del tomorrow night. Can't quite believe it, but hope it lasts.

It was not like Del to persist in the face of rejection. He appeared to be extroverted, self-confident, almost cocky at times. He had a ready joke for any occasion, and people liked his friendly manner and sense of humor. He had a sharp wit—sometimes too sharp. His humor sometimes had a hint of the cynic in it, sarcasm even. What he thought was good-natured joking, or teasing, could sometimes be rather barbed. He would not have suspected that it appeared that way. Indeed, he was painfully shy and unsure of himself in any social situation and used his pointed jokes and ready sense of humor to masquerade it. It generally worked well for him. He was well-liked, and enjoyed his role as Student Council President and the other responsibilities that resulted from that.

In spite of his popularity, his shyness and lack of confidence where social interaction was concerned kept him distanced from people. Until he had started going steady with his current girl friend, he had dated very little. If he asked a girl for a date and she declined for any reason, he would immediately conclude she had no interest in him and that was that.

But he had persisted with Colleen. She had turned him down—twice. Normally, that would have been the end of it. But he had tried a third time, asking her to go to the Sophomore Class play. It was on a weeknight, and David would not be in town. This time, she had accepted. Her chemistry class was increasingly difficult and demanding, and she was afraid of missing a night's study time. But she didn't want to risk turning him down again.

April 17, 1956

Man! What a date! Del took me to the sophomore play. Afterward, we went to the drive-in, but were too late to get in. So we drove to the side road and watched from there. I would never have believed this Del was behind all that sarcasm. I like to never got him to take me home. He even kissed me! Lots of times!!

April 18

Del was a stranger again at school, but came by tonight and was a swell guy again. I sure like him—after two years of curiosity.

Just as the two masks of Tragedy and Comedy depict the theater, his two reactions to her defined him. At the play, he was so thrilled to be with her, to be seen with her, that he was nervously self-conscious. He sat beside her, wondering if any of the gang was noticing. He tried to be polite, proper—it was, after all, a first date. He would lean over and whisper his little jokes occasionally during the play, and she would smile. Then, it was over. He didn't know for sure what he should do, and wondered if he should take her home.

He didn't want the date to be over. Couples would often go to the small restaurant uptown for a Coke after dates. But in truth, he wanted to be alone with her. He asked if she minded taking in the second feature at the drive-in. She worried about being out too late. Chemistry was wearing her down, but she didn't want to say no. So they went.

His lack of confidence, his inability to risk the possibility of rejection, had always inhibited him. But not that night. Alone with her, he gave in to feelings for her with an abandon that surprised them both. She hadn't enticed him—but she didn't resist him. And the first time he kissed her it was as though she unlocked a door to something in him even he didn't know was there.

The next morning, in the bright light of day and with others watching, his emotional guards were all in place again. Many years later he told her, "I wish I had come up to you that morning, had smiled at you, and just said, 'Wow!'"

He hadn't done that. Instead, he was guarded, distant. His intrinsic insecurity took command. How could he know what she had felt about the evening? Maybe she let all her dates kiss her, like she did him. Maybe it didn't mean a thing. If he was too presumptuous, and she rebuffed him, it would be humiliating. So he put up his shield of self-protection. To make matters worse, in a small country town a boy's worst nightmare was to be seen in public showing affection for a girl. Word always got around town and the farmers teased them without mercy, making their life a misery of embarrassment and humiliation. A boy quickly learned that you didn't let yourself be seen in public looking like you liked a girl.

He felt embarrassed about it. He knew he was handling it badly, but couldn't seem to keep it from happening. So he hid behind that shield of learned self-protection all day—and made her wonder what was wrong. She didn't know why he was suddenly so distant. She thought he had really enjoyed their date together. Had he just used her? She was troubled all day, and relieved when he came that night and seemed like the Del she knew, again. In the privacy of her home, out of the glare of public awareness, he could be himself.

April 19, 1956

Del sure is attentive. It's sure a new feeling. Comes to meet me after Clothing class, and meets me every noon. Stays around in morning, talking. So nice. Fun!!

April 20, 1956

Del found out I wasn't going home for the weekend, and asked me to go to drive-in. OK! We sat through whole thing, till it closed. Home at 12:15. Had heart-to-heart talk till 1:25.

After nearly two years of studying together, of talking casually and working on projects together, after two years of mutual curiosity and with barely a month remaining before graduation, they were finally coming to know each other. And on a second date, they were having a "heart-to-heart" talk.

April 22, 1956

David came down this weekend. At first, I didn't want him to come. Then we went to a movie and made up, and it seemed like all the old feelings were still there. But I know Del could run him a close second—if I would let myself let him.

April 27, 1956

Del took me to Chorus Concert tonight. I had a solo—"Mr. Wonderful." I did fair, I guess. Afterward, to drive-in, then parked out by his folk's farm and talked. Not in till 1:00AM. He sure is a lot of fun. He seems so much like David, to me. I feel so much at home with him.

April 30, 1956

Back to grind in chemistry, trying to catch up. It's a holy terror!! Only two more experiments to go. Del in tonight to work on Prophecy. He certainly likes me!

May 3, 1956

I've learned so much today, and I'm sure messed up. Had Chorus trip to my high school. I sang solo, and they clapped and clapped. Made me sing it again. My folks were there. Del was with me. We went out to my folks for a while, then over to his place. Out to eat, then went to drive-in. On way home he let me know that he would like to marry me, someday. And I'm for the idea—I think. What about David? I'm crazy. This must be a fling.

Two weeks and two days had passed since their first date. During those sixteen days they had four dates. Outside the classroom, they had spent fewer than twenty-four hours together—and Del shocked her by telling her he hoped to marry her. Even more shocking, she realized she was in favor of the idea.

Why didn't she nip such talk in the bud, tell him that she liked him and enjoyed dating him, but that she was committed to David? In spite of all their conflicts, she still assumed they would marry after college. She had backed away from Rob when he got too serious—why not Del? And why did Del tell her such a thing? He had turned nineteen just a few months before. He had never even thought about marriage. His future plans went only so far as an engineering degree. He took it for granted that he would get married—to somebody, someday. But that day and that person had always been hypothetical, something that would happen sometime in the dim future.

They left each other that night knowing that something had happened between them. She could not deny that she was feeling something she had not even remotely expected to feel. She had simply wanted to date and have fun. She hadn't counted on this. But she also knew that first and foremost in her life was her degree. She was going to finish college. If she could not let David interfere with that, even at the risk of losing him, how could she take a chance on someone else? Would she do the same thing to him?

May 5, 1956

Worked all day and my mind was in total chaos every minute of it. Lordy—I keep wanting to forget David. Del fits me so exactly. But do I really want him, or just think I do?

May 6, 1956

I fear I'm falling in love. Really! With a guy who wants a farm house with a big picture window and a porch we can sit on and listen to the night. We were at my folks a while—rode horses. Then over to his folks. His brother and his old girl friend were there— looks like I don't have to worry about her anymore. After supper to drive-in, then parked, and just talked and talked and talked.

May 8, 1956

What a horribly mixed up day! As of today I've decided I'm following Del to K-State. Also, today David called, and came down. I guess it's truly over between us. He loved me, but I guess I didn't really love him. This eve Del and I worked like mad people to finish the Prophecy, and the Moments to Remember. Home, and we talked about an hour about lots of things. Sure funny how he fits me.

May 15, 1956

I don't know how it can change. How after nearly six years David can become an outsider—but he is. And Del has stepped in just all of a wonderful sudden. And he's a Del I never suspected existed. It's a thrilling thing, but so right. I feel most two-faced, but it's so.

It had been three weeks and five days since their first date. She had not been prepared for it, hadn't seen it coming. She had come to JuCo wanting to experience all the fun and excitement of college, and dedicated to her goal of getting her degree. But leaving David and falling in love with a total stranger was a possibility that she could not have imagined, much less believed could happen. Barely a month earlier, Rob had made it clear that he loved her and hoped to marry her. She had made it just as clear to him that David would always be her guy. Now, a month later, and after six years with David, she is accepting the fact that she has fallen in love with and will probably marry someone she had never expected to get to date. It was almost more than she could grasp.

And now, she had suddenly changed her plans to attend the teachers college and was going to the university with Del while he finished his engineering degree. She had been unwilling to risk that with David—but rationalized it by recognizing that Kansas State University had a nationally renowned home economics department.

May 17, 1956

David and I are truly through. My "puppy love" is over. His feelings were real, and mine weren't. Will I ever find the real thing? Is it really Del? I wish these next two years were over, and I'd marry Del in two weeks. I'm afraid this same thing will happen to us. Do I really have feelings? I never seem to let myself go. Will I ever get married, and have kids?

She was excited about her new love, and all that was happening to her. But she was also afraid. Afraid that she would let her new love for Del make it impossible to resist marriage, and she would lose her lifetime dream of a college degree. But she was even more afraid of herself. Afraid that she would let her obsession with a college degree drive a wedge between her and Del, as it had with David. Even worse, she was afraid that she would never let herself give in to her feelings and marry the man she loved, have his children and a life with him. With no husband, no family, a degree in home-making would be an empty prize, almost a mockery.

May 23, 1956

Last day of JuCo. Spent most of it with Del, getting yearbooks signed. Tonight was Commencement. I rated number two in our graduating class! Afterward Del and I parked north of town. We traded rings and are officially going steady. Never thought I'd do that in college. Del and I not in until 3:00 AM.

Her two years of JuCo had ended. Although she and David had gone together for all four years of high school they had never exchanged rings, nor did they do so during her two years of JuCo. They had never discussed it. They also both took it for granted they would get married after finishing college, but had never really discussed that, either. Nevertheless, she had arrived at the junior college with her life planned, all mapped out. She would study hard, date a little, have a little fun, graduate, go to the state teachers college, finish her degree in Home Economics, graduate and marry David. They would have three children and live happily ever after.

Now, it was over. She had studied hard, harder than she thought possible. She had dated a little, and had lots of fun. JuCo had been hard, far harder than she had feared. True to form, she had succeeded beyond her dreams, academically, graduating second in her class—ahead of Del. But sixteen days of the last two months at JuCo had turned her plan for her life on its head. She had decided to go to K-State, where Del was planning to attend, instead of the teachers college. They had exchanged class rings and were going steady—something she had vowed to herself she would not do while in college. She now knew in her heart, as well as her mind, that she would marry, not David, but the guy whose ring she was now wearing—a guy with whom she had her first date just five weeks earlier. It was more than she could grasp.

She did go to work that summer at the chemical company, down at the teachers college. Del ran his own contract hay-baling business, living at his parents' farm. They missed each other terribly, but wrote constantly and called long-distance for a few minutes when they felt they could afford it, or were too lonely to resist it. They were together on most weekends. Del would drive down to see her, or she would find a ride home. It seemed to her too much like it had been with David, and she worried about it. But through those three summer months their feelings for each other solidified. They felt they were meant for each other, destined to be together.

As before, as it had been with David, she was concerned about the next two years. How would they handle the conflicting demands of college and their desire to be together? She was still afraid she wouldn't be able to handle college and marriage, but didn't think they could wait two years. They talked it through during the summer and decided they should get married the following summer, after their first year at the university. She hoped she could handle one year of being married and being in college, if it was their last year. But it didn't work out that way. They started classes in September of that eventful year. At the end of January, at the end of their first semester, they were married at his home church.

In most respects, being married while in college proved to be even more difficult than she had feared. But they would not have wanted it any other way. It took longer than they had planned. They had no financial assistance, and the need to work part time forced them to reduce their class loads. But two years almost to the day after they were married Colleen graduated Magna Cum Laude, seventh in her class of nearly five hundred, with a Bachelor of Science degree in Home Economics—and her straight-A minor in chemistry. Del had started in Agricultural Engineering, but later changed to Electrical Engineering, setting him back. He graduated Cum Laude eighteen months later.

In another strange twist of fate, Del's brother had shown an immediate interest in Del's former girl friend when Del had started dating Colleen. They started dating within days of when Del and Colleen started dating, and were married just two months after Del and Colleen were married. The four of them remained close over the years, and shared golden wedding anniversary celebrations fifty years later.

Chapter 2

Epiphany

It could have ended there. We met, fell in love, got married and lived "happily ever after." We'd sit in our rocking chairs, reminisce over our Golden Anniversary album, and let the rest of the world go by. End of story.

But it didn't happen that way. As our three children, and their peers, matured and began to get married, things started going wrong. Something seemed to be happening to marriage. Attitudes were changing, the wheels starting to come off the marital bandwagon. And I began to have experiences that conspired to compel me to look anew at marriage in general, and my own marriage in particular.

I can't point to a specific date or a particular experience and say, "Aha! That's when I first became aware that marriage was in trouble, in our society." But when I got married, marriage was the norm for society. Although divorce was not unheard of, it was unusual. And living together, outside of marriage? Shacking up? Well! That was indeed unacceptable. Today, that is all being turned on its head. Something has, in fact, drastically changed in what the National Marriage Project of Rutgers University, in its 2007 Annual Report on Marriage, calls "the state of our unions."

If I were to try to identify the first time I was forced to acknowledge that our societal attitudes regarding marriage were shifting, I might have to choose the time when my older brother related an experience he had while riding on an elevator.

Several years ago he was sharing an elevator with a high-school-age girl. How they happened to get on the subject, I don't recall that he said. But as the floors dinged by, he happened to mention to her that he had been married for over forty years. And what was her reaction? Did she express awe, and admiration? Did she congratulate him for such an accomplishment? No, she said nothing of the sort. Incredulous, she replied:

"Forty years? To the same person? How boring!"

It wasn't what he expected, and I don't remember how he said he responded. He probably didn't, since her response was so unexpected.

How boring?

I could have speculated on several possible responses from the girl, but that would not have been among them. In fact, even after giving it a fair amount of thought, I still don't know exactly how I would have responded to her. I guess my primary reaction has been to wonder: at what point in our society did marriage become a form of entertainment?

"Hey, honey, you wanta go see a movie? Or, we could get married, for a while."

Her comment did have one beneficial effect, for me at least, in that it served as an impetus to start me thinking about my own marriage. I'm not sure what, at the tender age of twenty-and-a-half, I expected marriage to be but I don't think I expected to be "entertained." I think I expected to be—well, married. That was pretty much the point of it. I did know that I was head-over-heels crazy over a really cute blond, and I couldn't conceive of spending my life any way other than with her. That it might prove to be boring never entered my mind.

So, as I thought about it, I couldn't help but feel sorry for that young girl—and her unfortunate, future short-term husband—who considered marriage to be just some form of competition for *American Idol* or *Entertainment Tonight*.

Sad to say, she may simply have stated, in typical teen-ager hyperbole, what too many have come to accept. That is, the traditional marriage vow in which we claim that we will be married for the rest of our life appears to be, for far too many newlyweds today, a romantic ideal but not something they necessarily expect to experience themselves, or perhaps even want to experience.

Another personal experience, that occurred three years before our fiftieth anniversary, had the deepest effect on me and was the most influential in eventually causing me to write this book. I believe it will be helpful in understanding my perspective in later chapters if I relate that experience in some detail.

I assume it was obvious in the previous chapter that we believed we were destined for each other, that ours was a storybook romance. But every story has to have some "tension" in the plot to carry it along and, as happens to most marriages, our storybook romance developed times of tension.

There is a line from an old movie—I believe it was *Best Friends*, starring Burt Reynolds and Goldie Hawn, but don't hold me to it—that we could sometimes relate to. In the movie, Burt's character is talking to the mother of the girl he is about to marry. She offers him her one-liner philosophy of life: "You see, honey, life just sometimes has a way of kicking the s--t out of you." There were times during our marriage when that seemed all too real, when the myriad stresses of earning a living and raising a family in modern society felt rather overwhelming. That, and the routine nature of living life on a daily basis, eventually pushed our storybook romance into the past.

I suppose it's only natural. When you are first falling in love, every feeling and emotion is new and exciting. Each thing you learn about the other is a new discovery, that makes your new love seem more exciting and brings you even closer. Every moment apart is filled with longing and anticipation for the time when you'll be together again. It is a time marked by infatuation and euphoria. But as years begin to pass in your marriage, that newness naturally wears off. Routine begins to replace romance.

It is difficult to describe exactly what changes over the years. I have two candid snapshots taken of Colleen and me that I find rather amusing, but that relate to the point. The first was taken just a few days after we were married. We were visiting my parents, and I was sitting on a chair, lacing up my hunting boots. Colleen was sitting near me. She was looking at me so adoringly that apparently someone thought it worthy of a picture. We don't remember who took it, but have laughingly dubbed it "The Adoration of Del" (I hope Da Vinci will excuse our little plagiarism).

The second picture was taken at Christmas, just a month before our nineteenth wedding anniversary. Colleen and I were sitting together on a sofa at her parents' house, unwrapping gifts. Apparently I was telling her something about one I had just opened. But we were looking at each other so intently that, again, someone apparently decided it was worth a snapshot. I had written on the back of the picture,

> "If we can still look at each other like this after nineteen years of marriage, I guess we must be doing something right."

After nearly twenty years, the feelings of infatuation and excitement of when we first fell in love, when Colleen could look at me adoringly while I was putting on my boots, had faded. But it was obvious from the second picture that the love had not. Nevertheless, the feelings do change.

Except for the occasional "fuss," as Colleen called our disagreements and disputes, we got along well and always enjoyed each other's company. We remained close, had no major conflicts, and never felt the marriage was threatened. Neither of us ever felt that the other no longer loved them. Indeed, we often agreed that ours was one of the better marriages of all the couples we knew.

In spite of that, as years turned into decades, I guess I would have to say that our marriage, and our relationship, became so familiar to me that I let the routine nature of life cause me to stop thinking much about it, at least very often. Our lives were caught up in the day-to-day routine and demands on our time and emotions. The feelings of excitement and euphoria, of being head over heels in love, that attach to a new relationship and that I had felt so intensely when first married faded into the past. I would imagine that our experience is quite common among married couples.

But then one morning that all changed. In 2004 we were to attend our fiftieth high school reunions, and had pulled out our old yearbooks and photo albums to reminisce. As I was flipping through the pages of one of the albums, one winter morning long before sunrise, I came to a particular picture from our wedding. It was a typical cast-of-characters picture with the bride and groom surrounded by parents, maid of honor, best man and all the others. The small-town minister was standing behind us, looking pious and officious. I was smiling, looking happy but rather dazed.

Standing beside me in the picture was this beautiful young girl, looking out at me across fifty years with sparkling eyes, her face radiantly happy. I had seen that picture plenty enough times before. We have a copy on our bedroom fireplace mantle. But when I saw it this time, something different and unexpected happened. Suddenly, all those feelings I had experienced decades earlier surged through me again, as real as they had been the moment the shutter clicked. I had the good fortune to get to experience "falling in love" all over again with the girl I married.

It's been a strange experience. I suppose we all would like to get to relive our youth, in some fashion. But I never had reason to believe that after half a century of marriage a person could suddenly feel about his wife the way he did at age nineteen, when they were first dating. It's not exactly the same, of course. When you first start dating you don't know each other. There is an excitement associated with discovering your mutual attraction, your feelings for each other, and the sense of amazement that she could feel about you the way you feel about her. We say we are "nuts about each other," that "we're crazy about each other." Certainly, that's the way the feelings make us act.

After fifty years, you know pretty much all there is to know about each other, so the euphoria and excitement of discovery can't be the same. There can't be the same sense of magic and disbelief. But there was, or is, in place of that something even deeper and more meaningful. I've wondered about it quite a bit, since that epiphanous moment of resurgence. How do you "fall in love" with someone you've loved for most of your life? And why did it occur, when it did? I wondered if others have experienced the same thing.

In reflecting on it all, it seems to be multi-faceted. First, I was reminded, while looking at our wedding picture, just how overwhelmed I was back then that this girl who had so captivated me had fallen for me and had agreed to marry me. But now, there is also a deep sense of humility and appreciation that a person you are so strongly attracted to would be willing to commit themselves to you, completely and wholeheartedly, for the rest of their life. That is rather awe-inspiring, when you think about it. At the time you take your vows and make that pledge, it seems rather theoretical. But now, fifty years later, it is accomplished fact. You realize how deeply it makes you feel about someone who would do that for you.

Another aspect of the experience was the recognition of just how lucky I was in the choice I made for a life partner. It seems rather unfeeling, or certainly unromantic, to say it, but in some respects marriage seems to be a bit of a "crapshoot." That is, we won't know for sure how our choice for a spouse is going to turn out for quite some time after the wedding. It takes time, sometimes years, for a person's real personality to exert itself on a relationship.

There's an old saying to the effect that "the older you get the more like yourself you become." As we age, it becomes increasingly difficult to put up the false fronts that we may be willing to do earlier on, or to concede our wills and desires to those of another person—even if it is your spouse. As the years roll by it is not uncommon to see a person appear to change from what they had been. Colleen and I are surprised at how much different some of the people we know are now, from the kind of person we thought they were years ago. Some of them seem to be less tolerant and more critical than they appeared to be when we first met them. That's not always true, of course. But if you made a poor choice in a marriage partner, several years may pass before you are forced to accept that fact.

In my case, the longer I am married the more I realize how fortunate I was. Colleen and I had our differences and occasional problems, but I can't imagine someone being better suited for me in all the important ways than she was—and is. So part of the rebirth of feelings came about, I think, from the realization that the fates and God had truly smiled on me fifty years ago.

Looking at our wedding picture that morning also made me realize how grateful I am. Thank God, thank fate, thank your lucky stars. Thank whatever you believe is responsible for guiding our lives in the directions they take. But in the face of the problems suffered in their marriages by so many we know, and the failures of those marriages, I had to acknowledge how blessed and fortunate I have been in my own.

I suppose that all that I have described above is the basis for why getting married, and staying married, seem so important to me, now. We don't get to have very many truly one-of-a-kind emotional experiences in our lives. Birth of a child, some religious experience, or a near-death experience, perhaps. But recognizing, and comprehending, that a person could care so deeply for you that they literally devote their life to you is certainly such an experience.

I've never turned seventy before. I don't know if every man experiences this same resurgence of feelings that I've described above. Maybe it's simply nostalgia, or that I am now having to face my own mortality. Maybe every man has this renewal of feelings as he approaches the winter of his life. Maybe not. I just give thanks that I got to experience my golden wedding anniversary feeling like a newlywed. The experience and the feelings that have resulted from it have caused me to give a lot of thought to my marriage, and to marriage in general. It has also caused me to think a lot about what happens to people over the years of a marriage—and to the reasons why marriages succeed and why they fail.

The late Scott Peck began his best-seller book *The Road Less Traveled* with a blunt admonition: "Life is difficult." As any married couple will attest, sometimes so is marriage. Life is not slow pitch—there are lots of fastballs and change-ups thrown at you. It is not always easy for a couple to deal with those problems, as well as each other, year after year without it taking a toll.

Unfortunately, it seems our society does little to help. Too much of our culture today diminishes marriage, fidelity, loyalty to one person. Celebrities trade partners more often than most of us trade cars, and receive constant adulation from a swooning media and public for doing so. Lust has become a synonym for love. The self-esteem movement places self above selflessness. In the face of this corrosive onslaught against the whole concept of marriage and fidelity, when problems seem overwhelming and your partner seems all too familiar, it's easy to wonder, *Who needs this?* Perhaps it is not surprising, then, that marriages struggle and oftentimes fail.

The problems associated with marriage are always with us. They are trumpeted in the tabloids by celebrities who make a mockery of marriage. Our friends, our own children, struggle and often divorce. I suppose that is why the resurgence of feelings that swept over me that morning felt almost like a religious experience, not unlike the Christian experience of being "born again."

I don't know how a person could experience those feelings without having gone through your lives together. That is why, I now believe, it is so essential that a couple stay married "for life." I've had a couple of friends, guys who have also had their golden anniversaries, or soon will have, who have commented about having the same sort of realization about their own marriage.

It has created in me a perspective, a sense of gratitude and appreciation, that can only come after a life together. I've always believed in marriage, and would not have wanted to spend my life any other way. But I had no way of anticipating the reward of the feelings of closeness and satisfaction that Colleen and I are now experiencing as a result of a lifetime of marriage. Those feelings influence everything I have to say throughout this book.

The coup de grace, the thing that happened to me that set me firmly on the path to writing this book, happened during our fiftieth anniversary celebration event. I was visiting with a young friend of my son. The young man had recently gotten married, and was congratulating Colleen and me on our marital longevity. He told me that he had read that of all the couples that get married only three percent celebrate a golden anniversary together, and that he was most impressed that we had done so.

That passing comment really set me on my heels. Could that really be true, that only three percent of marriages now make it to fifty years? Perhaps he misunderstood something he read, maybe he was mistaken.

I wanted to find something to refute it—or worse, confirm it—so set out to do a little of my own research. I found a U.S. Department of Commerce report, dated February 8, 2002, that led me to a report by the U.S. Census Bureau. It is chock-a-block full of statistics on marriage and divorce in these United States, as of 1996. If you're interested in the gory details, it is available on the Web.

But buried within the report are three interesting statements:

- The number of men and women who marry at least once by age sixty is approximately ninety-five percent.

- The probability of future divorce from a first marriage was about fifty percent for males ages 25 to 30 in 1996.

- About 52 percent of currently married couples had reached at least their fifteenth anniversary in 1996, but only five percent of them had reached their golden anniversary (50 years).

So my young friend's figure of three percent was perhaps a little pessimistic, but "close enough for government work." However, given that the five percent figure was from more than a decade earlier, and given the trend line, my friend's three percent figure is probably rather accurate.

I don't mean to turn this into a college course on statistics, but those three statements include an intriguing paradox. What the Census Bureau seems to have learned with their interviews and analyses is that Americans want to be married—or at least they apparently want to get married, if by age sixty virtually every one of us will have married at least once.

Why that is so is open to dispute and opinion, but I personally believe that we are genetically programmed to seek a mate. I believe it is ingrained in us, that it is our very nature as human beings. But it goes far beyond a simple evolutionary force to perpetuate the species. The birds and the bees do that, but they don't get married (actually, some in the animal kingdom essentially do that; think of a lion pride). Monogamous marriage—taking a mate for life—has been the norm for civilizations for most of recorded history. The Old Testament of the Bible, written thousands of years ago, promotes it in a variety of ways. Matrimony is one of the seven sacraments of the Catholic Church. There has to be a reason for that. What we seem to need, what prior generations innately believed was best for us as individuals and as a civilization, is not to simply mate but to have a mate for life.

Indeed, two other salient facts were mentioned in the report that support my contention. The report found that "Most people who had ever divorced were now married," and further stated that the median time for a second marriage after a first divorce was less than three years. Apparently, we want to get married, and to be married—but we seem to have problems staying married.

It is the second two items of the three listed above that cause the paradox, the dilemma, in my mind. If, as I believe, we are genetically programmed to seek a life mate, to the extent that virtually all of us get married at some point in our lives, then why do so many of us now divorce? Why does only one couple in twenty, or even one in thirty, get to experience the reward and pleasure of a golden anniversary? And an even more perplexing question is, why do so many couples now shun marriage completely, choosing to live together with no commitment to each other?

What changed within our society? What happened during this span of my marriage? I don't really believe that people loved each other more in previous generations, than now. So what put the hole below the waterline of the marital ship of state?

In the following two chapters I offer three answers to that question. The rest of the book presents my beliefs regarding two fundamental questions on the subject. The first and most important question is, "What's so important about getting married—and staying married?" The second and perhaps the more difficult question to answer is, "So what does it take to have a good marriage—and to stay married?"

Chapter 3

So What's the Problem?

Based on the statistics presented in the previous chapter, it would appear that marriage is on trial in our society. The facts of the case, as is true for many cases that come to trial, are easy to state. The percentage of couples who get married has steadily decreased over the last forty years, the number per thousand declining by fifty percent since 1970. During that same period the number of couples who choose to cohabit before getting married has increased by nearly 1200% (no, that's not a misprint). The number of couples who cohabit with no intention whatsoever of getting married has also increased dramatically. Individuals are choosing to get married at a later age, and to have children at ever later ages. Many couples choose to remain childless.

The facts do not present a pretty picture for marriage and family, in this trial of lifestyles that is taking place daily in America. I offer no attempt to argue the facts. They are what they are. I have, however, expended considerable effort in an attempt to understand why they are what they are, but with little success. All the evidence suggests that a large percentage of males and females are coming into adulthood believing that marriage will not be beneficial to them. I've tried to understand why they believe that—again, with little success.

When Colleen and I stood before a minister, family and friends that January day in 1957 and vowed that we would be married "as long as you both shall live," we never questioned the presumption that we were, in fact, going to spend the rest of our lives together. We wouldn't have wanted it any other way, and it never entered our minds that we would not. But during these five decades we have watched divorce become not only more common, but virtually expected.

I believe that several fundamental cultural changes caused this tectonic plate shift in what once was the bedrock of our society, namely marriage. One of those changes was the development of the "me" phenomenon that started in the '60s and that has grown within our ranks over the ensuing decades. That this phenomenon contributed substantially to the decline in marriage was persuasively argued in the book *The Total Couple*, by Albert Lee and Carol Allman Lee, published in 1971.

The first chapter, "Family in Crisis," deals with the deteriorating state of marriage and what the authors considered to be the causes for that deterioration. They laid much of the blame at the feet of the growing "me" versus "us" phenomenon. The remainder of the book presents the authors' views on how a married couple could strengthen their marriage in the face of such problems.

It appears to only be getting worse. People today all too often see themselves, and their lives, in the context of "me," and not of "us." That is, they defer or even opt out of marriage because they want to get to experience more of life on their own, rather than "sacrificing" their life to that of a marriage. They place "me" before "us." The problem I have with that belief, or attitude, is deep and fundamental. I want to emphasize it here, because I believe it cannot be overstated.

The problem is this: Placing "me" before "us" defines marriage in terms of what will be lost in life, rather than in terms of what will be gained.

I cannot personally relate to that sentiment because I stopped thinking of my life in terms of "me" the night of my first date with Colleen, and thought only in terms of "us" from that night forward. Nevertheless, I have tried to understand the concerns of people who think of marriage in terms of what they will lose, rather than what they will gain. But, in truth, I don't understand them. I accept the fact that you have to defer some of your preferences to those of your mate, in marriage. It couldn't be otherwise. Fairness requires it. But I can't put that in a context of losing something.

In my attempts to understand this mindset, this sense of what you "lose" when you get married, I spent quite a bit of time thinking back over my own married life. I tried to imagine which part of my married life I would have been willing to give up, and of what I would have gained in its place, had I chosen to have more "me" time in my life.

I tried to imagine that I had waited until I was in my thirties, as is commonly done today, before I decided to get married. When I was thirty-five, I had a nine-year-old daughter, a seven-year-old son and a two-year-old son. I tried to imagine them not being in my life during those years. I tried to imagine not having held them on my chest as infants, letting them sleep while I read a book or had a cup of coffee. I tried to imagine not lying on the floor, playing with them as toddlers, or watching them evolve from little bundles to budding personalities. It didn't work. I in fact cannot imagine not having had those years, and having experienced those joys.

I also was forced to recognize that had I elected to not get married until I was thirty-five, I would not have Colleen in my life. We would have gone our separate ways when we graduated from the junior college where we met. I tried to imagine me not married to her. I tried to imagine her married to someone else, imagine me married to someone else. No way would that work.

Perhaps, then, I should have at least waited until after college to get married. I tried to imagine myself living in a fraternity, living the single life of Joe College, with getting plastered being the entertainment du jour. Then I remembered our nights helping each other through difficult courses and exams. I thought of the times Colleen comforted me when things had gone very badly. I remembered our Saturday nights of dressing up and going out to movies, or to the Student Union to relax and "people watch." Those were some of our hardest years together, but also in many ways some of our best.

Or maybe I would have been willing to give up our dreaming together of where we would choose to live after graduation, of what our life together was to become. Perhaps I could have given up the pride I felt as I watched my wife and best friend cross the stage in cap and gown, to receive the diploma for the degree that she had strived so long and hard to achieve.

No, I wouldn't have wanted to lose any of that. Then I looked at pictures of our grandchildren. Although our grandkids came along somewhat late in our marriage, compared to what some of our friends experienced, we are still young enough and healthy enough to get to experience their growing up, and to be a part of their formative years. How could I want to have missed that? "Grand" children are so named because of the terms that have evolved in our society to describe generational relationships. But the term is well-suited. They are grand. I never expected to get to feel about a child the way that I do about my grandchildren. It is a relationship entirely different from that with your own children. I don't know why. But I do know I would not have wanted to miss it.

As I engaged in all those mental gymnastics, I would often look at pictures of Colleen and me from when we first were dating, or newly married. They reminded me of all that we felt and shared at that embryonic stage of our life together. We were so caught up in each other, and felt so alive and had such a sense of anticipation of our life to come. I could not, and cannot, help feeling a sense of nostalgia, of wishing that we could once again experience those feelings.

Then, she would come and sit with me, and as we talked I would glance at those pictures from fifty years ago—and think how much better it is to feel the way I do now.

So, what is the answer? What part of my life did I sacrifice by choosing to become "us," instead of remaining "me?" What experience did I deprive myself of enjoying that would have surpassed all the ones I had while married, that would have made my life better in some way? What penalty did I incur for committing myself wholly and completely to Colleen, closing all the exit doors to any other life or person?

I'll repeat what I said above. In being allowed to mature in an environment that celebrates "me" in favor of "us," far too many people now view marriage in terms of what they will lose, rather than what they will gain. In a sense that was true for me. But what I lost by choosing to get married when I did was being half a person, with half a life. What I gained was the other half of me, and a life I could never have experienced alone.

It is truly unfortunate, I believe, that so many individuals are choosing to deny themselves that experience. They seem to be afraid they will miss something in life. But what they really miss is the best part of life.

I've accomplished a number of rather challenging and, I would claim, significant things in my life. But none of those things would now take precedence over, or seem more important than, my marriage. The committees and boards I chaired have long been forgotten. The certificates of appreciation are fading. But every morning Colleen still wants to know if I slept well, and how I'm feeling. Many nights I left her at home, alone with three small children, to attend those meetings. But she is the one who still cares about me, and for me. It is for that very reason that I am becoming increasingly concerned about what appears to be happening to our society's attitudes toward marriage, and especially to the belief in marriage "'til death do us part."

Okay, so it sometimes requires some sacrifice. It is oftentimes difficult. So what? Life is like that. And nothing, in my experience, will reward you in any way close to that of living life with your best friend, committed to each other through marriage.

I am going to go out on a limb, here, and suggest a second and even more fundamental cause of the problems that now seem to afflict marriage. It is purely conjecture on my part. I have seen no formal studies to support my contention, but plenty of evidence. That is, I strongly suspect that much of what happens to a couple today, that can ultimately lead to divorce, can be laid at the feet of the so-called self-esteem movement. Colleen and I have referred to it for years as the "me-first" attitude. It is interesting to me that the authors of *The Total Couple* attributed some of the growing problems of divorce to the "What's in it for me?" attitude. So perhaps I'm not alone out on that limb.

We first began to notice the effect years ago when we would take our kids to a movie, or to a playground, anywhere that kids might have to line up and take turns. Without exception, some of the kids would begin to try to push into the head of the line—"me first." It was a pervasive phenomenon that grew more noticeable with time. Some individuals appeared to believe that they had a birthright to come before others, that their interests were more compelling than those of others.

In more recent years that attitude evolved into the so-called self-esteem movement, in which it is considered that nothing is quite so important to a person as his opinion of himself. I read recently of schools that teach children to sing a little song to the tune of "Frere Jacques" called "I Am Special." Its first verse starts out as follows:

I am special,
I am special,
Look at me,
You will see,
Someone very special....

There is, of course, nothing intrinsically wrong with teaching children to believe in themselves. Self-confidence is essential to a healthy and productive life. But when a child is repeatedly told throughout their formative years that they are "special," when they are praised not for accomplishment but for merely trying, when they are congratulated for merely displacing water in the swimming pool, it can easily distort their impression of what will later be required of them to coexist with all the others they encounter in life—including all those who also believe in their own "special-ness."

Colleen showed me an article—"Do You Adore My Child As Much As I Do?"—in our local newspaper while I was working on the manuscript for this book. The point of the article was obvious from the title. The attitude I've discussed above could easily be paraphrased as "Do you adore me as much as I do?"

It may make a person feel quite special, at least for a while, but when it comes to having a happy and successful marriage this "I am special, me-first" mentality can only lead to problems. Simply stated, putting yourself ahead of your spouse is a recipe for failure in a marriage.

You may notice several references to movies sprinkled throughout these pages. That's because I have always enjoyed good movies, and they often speak to real life. You will also find references to passages from the Bible. I am a professing, and attempt to be a practicing, Christian. Our Christian faith was a strong component in our marriage. Obviously, I find the Bible to be a good guide for my life. But whether you are a Christian, of some other faith, or believe in none at all, I think you could agree that some of the teachings of the Bible can have a ring of truth. One such verse, from the Gospel of Mark, is apropos to what I have said above. I've used the Revised Standard Version of the New Testament, in which Jesus makes the statement:

> For whoever would save his life will lose it, but
> whoever loses his life for my sake...will save it.

In this particular verse, Jesus is referring to spiritual salvation, but the concept can clearly be applied to marital "salvation." The person who tries to "preserve his life," that is, who tries to put his own life first in the marriage, will lose the marriage. And the person who puts the life of his spouse, and of the marriage, ahead of his own will preserve his marriage.

These two cultural shifts of attitude—a developing sense of "me first," and a resultant growing unwillingness to subordinate yourself to another person—are affecting, and afflicting, life and marriage in ways that, frankly, I find rather scary. If you want to get a better picture of what I mean, do an Internet search on "marriage without children." You will find websites such as NoMarriage. com, and many others like it. The bitterness expressed in some of those websites, and the vituperation poured out on marriage, the nuclear family and the concept of legally committing yourself to another person for the rest of your life is enough to rattle your cage—or at least it does mine. They are painfully clear illustrations of the self-absorption that I mentioned above.

Colleen and I have seen too many young couples struggle in their marriages, and have seen too many of those marriages fail, because one or both of the couple could not seem to grasp the truth of that need to place your spouse ahead of yourself. No matter how much they may have believed they loved their mate, no matter how they tried to get along, in the final analysis they were unable to subordinate their personal interests to those of their spouse. Sooner or later, most of those marriages failed.

On the other hand, those marriages we have known that seemed to us to be the strongest and happiest were those in which both of the couple believed they received more than they gave. In other words, in being willing to "lose their life" for the sake of their spouse and their marriage, they in fact "saved their life," and their marriage. They each were willing to subordinate their interests to those of their spouse. As a result, it should not be surprising to learn that both of them felt they, in fact, got more than they gave in return. It's hard for a marriage to falter in that context.

In some respects, it could also be said to be a matter of convenience. We are steeped in convenience in our modern society, and demand it. Fast food, drive-thru windows, cell phones, the Internet, ATMs—everything in our society is in some manner predicated on convenience. Problem is, marriage oftentimes is not "convenient." To accommodate our spouse we must frequently inconvenience ourselves, and that oft-times does not go over real well in our self-esteeming society.

So, in fact, a lot really has changed during the span of my marriage. There is a third factor that now affects marriage that I believe must also be mentioned. That is the fact that our expectations of marriage have drastically changed. Our perceptions of what will be required of us in a marriage are now fundamentally different from those of previous generations. I discuss this issue in depth in the next chapter.

Chapter 4

After We Say "I Do"

Dr. Gary Chapman, a marriage counselor for more than thirty years, opens his book *The Five Love Languages* with a poignant story. While on a flight, a man in an adjacent seat learned of Dr. Chapman's profession and asked him a plaintive question: "What happens to the love after the marriage?" The man had been married three times, and in each of the marriages the intense feelings that had brought him into the marriage had eroded and been lost. All three marriages had ended in divorce. The man went on to ask Dr. Chapman,

> "Is my experience common? And those who don't divorce, do they learn to live with the emptiness, or does love really stay alive in some marriages? If so, how?"

What changes after we say, "I do?" We meet and fall in love. We get married and expect to live the dream of "happily ever after." Then if we are like the man on the plane, we eventually find ourselves lying awake some sleepless night, our feelings as black as the ceiling above, wondering, *What happened to the love?*

What *is* going wrong, that so many marriages fail, today? What *does* change, and *has* changed within us and our society? In my parent's generation, divorce was virtually unknown. In my own generation, and especially those following us, it seems to have become as common as dust on a knick-knack shelf. Something has dramatically changed in that short span of time. If divorce statistics are to be believed, that man's unfortunate experience is all too common. As puzzling as it is to me, I have no reason to doubt the statistics that I discussed earlier.

Colleen and I are surprised by, and concerned about, how many of those we know who are like the man in Dr. Chapman's story and have been unable to make a first, or even a second, marriage endure. We believe marriage not only should be, but in fact can be, a life commitment. Does that mean we believe divorce is wrong, or immoral? Not necessarily. Sometimes divorce is for the best, a merciful ending to an unviable situation. Or perhaps we were just lucky, and didn't have to confront the problems that cause so many marriages to fail? Hardly. We had to deal with differences in personality and approaches to life's problems virtually from the git-go. That will become evident in the experiences that I relate in later chapters.

What we do believe is that spending life together as man and wife is the best way to spend life. No friendship, no support group, no twelve-step program, no attempt to rationalize co-habiting can provide any feeling close to that of being able to enjoy a life committed in marriage to your "dear companion." Jonathan Edwards, who I discuss in later chapters, refers to his wife Sarah in that manner in a letter in 1746. (Emmylou Harris used the same expression in her song "My Dear Companion." Edwards was more eloquent, but Emmylou's song was more poignant.)

I've always liked the phrase "dear companion" for what it says about the marriage relationship. When you reach that point in life where the future feels much shorter than the past, nothing can compare to having a dear companion alongside you, one who has shared every joy and pleasure, every heartache and pain, and who knows you as no one else can.

Dr. Chapman in his book suggests that most couples who marry have a similar experience to that of his disconsolate fellow traveler. They fall in love, and expect that the intense feelings they share will last forever. Then, over a period of time after the wedding, reality sets in. He goes on to say:

> Little by little, the illusion of intimacy evaporates, and the individual desires, emotions, thoughts and

behavior patterns exert themselves....They fall
out of love, and at that point they either withdraw,
separate, divorce, and set off in search of a new
love experience, or they begin the hard work of
learning to love each other without the euphoria
of the in-love obsession.

Dr. Chapman claims that the "in-love obsession" typically
lasts no more than one to two years, in most marriages.

Colleen and I met and fell in love in every sense of the
sentiment described in Dr. Chapman's book. I think we were as
nuts over each other as most couples get to experience. Without
question, we felt the euphoria of the "in-love obsession." I'm not
certain what Dr. Chapman meant by the "illusion" of intimacy.
Nothing felt illusory about it for us, and I suspect most couples
feel the same when they first fall in love. And after our wedding,
reality did indeed set in, for us. Unlike the sad experience of the
man Dr. Chapman met on the plane, however, we did not "have to
learn to live with the emptiness." Quite the contrary.

I was also a bit puzzled by Dr. Chapman's contention that
the couple falls "out of love." I presume it depends on how being
"in love" would be defined. But I do understand his point. Over a
period of time, the euphoria wears off. Infatuation has to contend
with routine, and familiarity may not breed contempt but it can
take the edge off the excitement that was initially felt. When egos
and feelings have been battered by some pointless argument, it
is hard to remember what you felt on your first date. But I don't
consider that not being in love. When I took off on my hundredth
flight after getting my pilot license it was not nearly as exhilarating
as my first takeoff. That didn't mean I had stopped "loving" flying.
It only meant that I was emotionally adapted to it. I knew what it
was going to feel like. The newness of the feelings was gone.

It took a little probing to realize what Dr. Chapman meant by
his statement regarding "...the hard work of learning to love each
other without the euphoria of the in-love obsession." I generally
tend to think of work as being hard when it is unpleasant, when the

task at hand is an undesirable one. I do recognize, however, that work can be hard even if it involves something you enjoy doing. There may be difficult and challenging obstacles to overcome, but doing so makes the accomplishment more meaningful. Putting a man on the moon was hard work. Climbing Mt. Everest is hard work. Learning to say you're sorry when you know darn well you're in the wrong and don't want to admit it is hard work. But the result is undeniably worth the work.

And that did apply to us. We quickly learned that we each had personality traits that caused us, and for that matter occasionally still cause us, difficulties. We are both strong-willed, and tend to be a bit what our farmer-parents would have called "bull-headed." Our disagreements, our arguments, were oft-times more a tug-of-war in which we each tried to drag the other over to our point of view than they were an attempt to understand and find compromise. That's where we usually would wind up—understanding, and compromising. But getting there was sometimes a struggle.

Learning to cope with those differences, and learning to get past the hurt feelings, was sometimes difficult. I suppose you could have called it hard work. But I don't interpret that to mean that we were having to "learn to love each other." The statement puzzles me, in a sense. Why would you make the effort to better understand each other, if you didn't already love each other? I recognize that learning to get along with someone you don't like is a good policy for life in general, but it's hardly the way I view marriage.

Still in all, there is nothing new about any of that. Our parents, their parents, all generations of married couples, have had to learn how to get along with each other after the wedding. They, too, had problems but they rarely got divorced. If a married couple experiencing problems isn't anything new—if that hasn't changed—then what has? Why was the poor soul talking to Dr. Chapman on the plane thrice divorced?

Is marriage more difficult now than it was for earlier generations? When you reflect on the harsh realities of daily life in the days before all our modern conveniences, it is hard to believe that marriage had to endure under less stress then than it does now.

Nevertheless, something did change. The authors of the book *The Total Couple* traced the developing crisis in marriage to the attitude of "What's in it for me?" that came out of the Sixties, and to the uncertainties created by the feminist movements of that time. Traditional beliefs about love and marriage were being knocked akimbo, and many couples lost their moral and emotional compasses. I agree with much of that, but I also believe there is another contributor that wasn't mentioned. Perhaps it hadn't developed, then, to the degree that it has now.

I believe that a major contributor to today's divorce "epidemic" are the unrealistic expectations regarding love, and consequently marriage, that have been created by our celebrity-obsessed culture and popular media. I have no reason to believe that couples of my parents' generation loved each other any more when they got married than do couples today. Regardless, there is no doubt in my mind that my parents and earlier generations did go into marriage with different expectations and perceptions than is true today.

I believe, for starters, they were more realistic and pragmatic about what they were getting into and what would be required of them. Life was harsher then, in every respect, than it is now. The fact that being married wasn't all moonlight and roses was no different than was true for any other aspect of their life. So they were able to be more stoic, and accepting of the problems that inevitably confronted them in their marriages.

Conversely, I suspect many, if not most, young couples today in some way assume that when they get married those feelings of infatuation that come from first falling in love will continue on, indefinitely. Then, as Dr. Chapman says, when those feelings dissipate—and they inevitably do, sometimes rather quickly after the wedding—rather than accept it as part of life, the couple feels betrayed and lost. For earlier generations, I believe the basis for marriage was far more economic than it was romantic, so they didn't feel so bereft and puzzled when the "honeymoon was over."

In many respects marriage then was a matter of necessity, or even of survival. In the first place, prior to World War II, there was no real place for a woman in the work force. She had virtually no prospect for economic independence. Marriage was essential to survival, as was the need for children. With none of the modern conveniences of kitchen appliances, prepared foods and off-the-rack clothes, simply feeding and clothing the family was a full-time job for a wife and however many daughters there might be. When my Mom wanted to have fried chicken for dinner, she couldn't send one of us kids out to visit "The Colonel" to bring home a bucket of it. She had to start by having one of us catch the chicken and kill it, so it could then be scalded so feathers could be plucked, then it was cleaned, pin feathers singed off, cut up and, finally, fried.

Prior to World War II, the majority of Americans lived on farms, and running a farm was usually a ten to twelve hours a day, six days a week grind (seven, if you include the fact that the dairy herd had to be milked morning and evening every day, including the Sabbath) for the husband and as many sons as they might have.

It would not have been particularly surprising then, after a few months of this sort of demand on their time and energy, for those couples to wake up before sunrise some frigid winter morning in a dark, unheated house and realize that the "euphoria of the in-love experience" had been lost. For good or ill, they had each other and knew they were each completely dependent on the other. So unless their mate was unrepentantly dour and unpleasant, the marriage met their fundamental expectations. I know, from observing some of my relatives, that they still loved each other through "thick and thin." But I believe it was love based on different expectations than is true today.

That all began to change during World War II. Many women were hired into industry to replace the men who were being called into the military. Then, when the men came home, those women began to realize that they didn't want to give up their jobs and the economic independence. Soldiers came home keenly aware that there was a lot more to life than milking cows and hauling manure. The gals didn't want to stay home and be "Suzy Homemaker," and the guys didn't want to stay "down on the farm."

The whole structure of our society was changed in fundamental ways by those developments. Women were working, and didn't want the encumbrance of kids to raise. Men were busy at jobs in industry. Daughters weren't needed in the house, and sons weren't needed in the fields. In the absence of economic necessity as a basis for it, our perception of marriage began to change. No longer did a couple get married for economic survival.

As a result, marriage dynamics have completely changed. For my parents the formula was simple and well understood. You met someone you cared for, got married, then and only then had children, provided for them, and then looked forward to getting to enjoy your grandchildren at least a few years before you died or became too infirm. And if a girl hadn't gotten married by age eighteen, or so, "spinster" and "old maid" began to be her new first name. If the guy wasn't gainfully involved in earning a living, and married, by his early twenties "irresponsible" would often appear in sentences involving his name. Like it or not, people had to mature and take on the role of adult at a far younger age.

As an example of the changing attitudes about marriage, Colleen and I had to laugh at an entry in her mother's diary about the day she and Claude, Colleen's dad, got married. We found the diaries while going through personal belongings after her mother had died. In the diary, on the day of their wedding, her mother had written that she and Claude had helped catch a calf that had got out, and then later in the day picked up a couple of friends, drove to a town across the Missouri border, and got married. They came back home that night and told Claude's parents that they were now married, but didn't have the nerve to tell her parents until a day, or two, later.

Contrast that with marriage today. After World War II, marriage began to be romanticized. And in many respects that started in the Fifties, when Colleen and I got married. Many movies then featured a dewy-eyed Doris Day swooning over handsome Rock Hudson, and the plot was all about how she let him pursue her until she had caught him. Now this romanticizing of love and marriage has evolved to the point that a guy can't simply ask his girl to marry him. It has to be done in a supremely romantic, and often very public, setting.

Skywriters write the proposal across the heavens. It is requested on the Jumbotron at a football game half-time, with network cameras zoomed in on the dumb-struck object of the guy's affection. Spectators jump to their feet for a standing-O, as she mouths, "Yes!!!" and they kiss each other. Many a guy's knee gets dampened in the sand of a California beach as he kneels to ask for the hand of his beloved, as the sun sets in splendor over Santa Catalina Island. I get the impression, at times, that it has become some form of competition to see who can arrange the most original and supremely romantic setting for a proposal.

Naturally, the event itself, the wedding, had to keep pace, and most weddings now appear to be an attempt to approximate that of Princess Di. I've seen photographs of recent weddings where there were more attendants lined up at the front of the church than there were people in the pews, or so it appeared. Is it any wonder, then, that a couple might go into marriage with grossly exaggerated expectations of a lifetime of moonlight walks on white-sand beaches?

So, is all that a bad thing? Am I making light of such romantic beginnings to a marriage? Do I disapprove in some old-fashioned, tut-tutting sort of way? No, not really. In some respects I envy them. I sometimes wish I had created a more romantic setting for when I formally asked Colleen to marry me, and gave her an engagement ring. I could hardly have been more pragmatic about it.

But Colleen didn't care, or at least she so insists. I had told her barely two weeks after our first date that I wanted to marry her, and we had agreed within a few weeks that we were going to get married the following summer. It was entirely a question of how we could best fit a wedding into our college schedules and finances. By the time I gave her a ring and made it official, our getting married was already an accepted fact by both of us. But if I am to believe what she wrote in her diary, that night, there is no doubt that she was just as excited and thrilled to receive that ring as can be true today, regardless of the setting.

Expectations regarding marriage are obviously different, today, than was true in earlier generations. Neither male nor female requires marriage for financial support or independence. We do not—at least statistically speaking—get married to have someone to cook and clean house for us, and to raise our kids. That's what take-out and maids and daycare are for. Although having a family is still a part of marriage for many couples, that is usually not the sole basis for the marriage and many couples now choose to remain childless.

If statistics are to be believed, couples now enter into marriage on the basis of the "euphoria of being in love" and, apparently, expect that euphoria to last indefinitely. When the cold water of real life gets dumped on that euphoria, when they have to start learning to get along together on a daily basis, it would appear that lots of couples are not prepared to deal with that shock.

All of which brings me back to the guy on the airplane. What exactly did he truly expect was going to happen after the honeymoon? "What happens to the love?" he asked. "Do they learn to live with the emptiness?"

Given all the changed dynamics and shifted paradigms mentioned above, I can see where he might be confused. But in truth, what did he think happened to the love? That it got lost with his loose change under the cushions on the couch? I am firmly convinced, by now, that love doesn't get "lost." Love gets eroded, destroyed, trammeled, pummeled, allowed to starve to death from lack of nourishment—but it doesn't get lost. My suspicions are that if that guy had really wanted to know what had happened to the love in his marriages, then he should have had a long talk with the guy he saw in the mirror while he was shaving.

One thing that inevitably changes, for any marriage, is our perception. Life becomes so preoccupied with living in the details of the day that such things too often became our reality. When we were first dating, I could only think of Colleen as that incredible girl who was going to marry me. After we had been married for a number of years, I found myself wondering if she had remembered that I had a school board meeting that night and would have supper ready when I got home (which, in fact, she usually did).

It was hard to remember the "euphoria of the in-love experience" while helping the doctor hold our screaming child so he could stitch up a cut, or while trying to keep the gnats and sweat out of my eyes while under the car, changing the oil. Life oftentimes got in the road of romance. That sort of thing is inevitable, unavoidable. We got preoccupied, and distracted—but we didn't "fall out of love."

There is another factor affecting marriages that seems to have changed during the last generation or two. I would be remiss to not mention it. That factor is simply this: Colleen and I never once thought of divorce as an option to whatever problems we might have been experiencing. We had no concept of not spending our lives together. Yet every young couple we have known in recent years who experienced difficulties in their marriage appeared to implicitly accept that their problems could lead to divorce—or at least one of the two of them did.

If divorce is never accepted as an option, then other solutions to problems in a marriage have to be found. The couple will have to seek those solutions until equitable ones are found. On the other hand, if failure—divorce—is accepted as an option, failure can appear to be the easiest way out of those problems. Divorce becomes self-fulfilling prophecy. Conversely, an unwillingness to accept anything other than a life together bonds a couple together strongly enough that they can take their marital ship through the occasional storm-tossed waters.

We both recognize that not every marriage can survive, nor probably should. We are all familiar with the old joke that "marriage is not a word—it's a sentence." In the days when divorce was an unspeakable scandal, too many times that was reality, not a joke. Too many couples were doomed to suffer a life sentence of being penalized for making a bad first choice for a marriage partner. It would have been a merciful thing to let such a mismatch die of natural causes and give two people a chance at happiness with someone better suited to them. That caveat aside, it is still our conviction that an unyielding confidence that neither will ever forsake the other is essential to a lasting marriage. With that foundation, virtually any problem can be solved and survived.

Mathematicians like to refer to the "necessary and sufficient conditions" for some mathematical concept to be true, or valid. In the following chapters I talk about the few fundamentals that I have come to believe, if not sufficient, are certainly necessary to having an enduring marriage. And by that I obviously don't mean that marriage is a burden that has to be "endured." I mean one that lasts the lifetime of the couple, and is satisfying to both. If you and your spouse meet these "necessary" conditions, I can virtually guarantee that you will be well down the road to being rewarded with a happy, life-time marriage.

But that is the "how-to" of marriage. What I hope comes through all these chapters is the "why-to," why I believe so strongly, after fifty-plus years of living the experience, that marriage is the single most important thing you can do for yourself in life, and that it can be the single most rewarding thing you can experience in life.

Chapter 5

Like First—Then Love

*Love is a
many-splendored thing...*

...or so the 1955 Oscar-winning movie, and its hit-parade feature song, by that name would have had us believe. We have a fascination, or perhaps even an obsession, in our society with the concept of "love." We write songs about falling in love, make movies about whether there is such a thing as "love at first sight," and produce thousands of books on the subject.

What doesn't get songs or books written about it is the concept of the more pragmatic "like." We don't read books about two people who fall in "like" with each other, or wonder if "like at first sight" is truly possible. Teen-agers use the term to interrupt virtually everything they say. But the concept of liking someone being a fundamental prerequisite to a lasting marriage is, like, rarely mentioned. But I now strongly believe that its absence will in all probability doom a marriage, regardless of how much "in love" a couple may feel they are when they first marry. This is my personal opinion, of course, but one which is well supported by those who have made a career of studying marriage and the factors that lead to its success or failure.

Dennis Prager, the well-known author, columnist and radio marriage counselor, wrote two columns ("If You're Thinking of Marrying," Parts I & II) based on his decades of experience of radio counseling and discussions regarding marriage. In those columns he asked twelve questions of a person who is considering marriage. Prager believes those twelve questions address the issues that are fundamental to the success of a marriage (as an aside, if you're planning on getting married, or even if already married, go through those twelve questions together—they will be quite revealing, I suspect). The first of those questions, and I assume from that the one he considers to be the most important, is: "Is the person your best friend, or at least becoming so?"

To this question, Mr. Prager offered the following:

> It is easy to find a lover. It is easy to get excited about a new person. But if you cannot say that the person you are considering marrying has become or is becoming your best friend, you need to figure out why before you decide to marry. This is probably the single most overlooked question among couples, especially young ones.

I wholeheartedly agree with Mr. Prager. It has taken me years to first perceive, and then to fully understand, the difference between liking your mate and loving your mate. But there are significant and fundamental differences.

I don't know if exaggeration is a legitimate debating technique, or not, but it is an effective means of making a point. It may appear that is what I am doing in this chapter, as I elaborate on the importance of liking your spouse as well as loving your spouse. The reason I do so is because I've come to believe that it is essential to a marriage—but from what I see of the couples who are struggling in their marriages, it is a concept that is not well understood or even acknowledged.

We all recognize that there is a difference between liking someone and loving them, but it's hard to define what those differences are. Ever the good engineer, I first went to the dictionary in an effort to form a distinction between them. According to my favorite old Random House Unabridged Dictionary:

> *Like:* To take pleasure in; to find agreeable, attractive; regard with favor; enjoy.

Love: Profoundly tender or passionate affection
for a person; sexual passion or desire; affectionate
concern for the well-being of others.

Definitions for both these terms used several column-inches of very small print in my dictionary. I tried to include the essence of each in the definitions above, but that is rather difficult to do so I offer the following two examples in an attempt to differentiate the two.

The first example is from a scene that occurred during the 1984 Academy Awards presentations. Sally Field had just won her second Best Actress Oscar, this one for *Places in the Heart*. As part of her acceptance speech she said,

"I haven't had an orthodox career, and I've
wanted more than anything to have your respect.
The first time I didn't feel it, but this time I feel
it, and I can't deny the fact that you like me, right
now, you like me!"

That line has become a source of parody over the years, and is often misquoted as the silly, "You like me! You really like me!" But her statement has two significant aspects. It isn't surprising that it was important to her that her peers respect her. I have included a separate chapter on respect, because it is so fundamental to a good marriage. The surprising element in her comment was the pleasure that she derived from simply knowing that her peers liked her. She didn't claim, or expect, that they love her—but it was important to her that they like her. Which again raises the question of just what are the differences between the two emotions.

The second example is a situation that has been featured on all too many TV newscasts, and seen in too many newspaper stories. A young man—a teenager, even—has been charged with a brutal crime, murder perhaps, and is on trial. The young man's mother is being interviewed, and is asked the inane question of how it all makes her feel. Her answer is stereotypically something like this:

"I can't condone what he did, and he has to suffer the consequences of it. But he's still my son, and I love him." The mother still loves her son—but she probably doesn't like him. There is a difference.

It would seem, then, that to like someone would be fairly simple and straightforward. You find them agreeable, attractive and you enjoy them. Love, on the other hand, may be a many-splendored thing, but it is also a far more complicated thing. First of all, there are so many variations of the emotion. The love that the mother of the son charged with murder feels is not the love that mother felt when her son was a newborn baby. And neither of those is the same love that a newlywed couple feels for each other—or for that matter, that a seventy-year-old feels for his wife of fifty years. Nor is that the same love as Mother Theresa felt for the poverty-stricken wretches of Calcutta.

We are saddled, in today's culture, with the incessant but misguided equating of sexual attraction to love. I seriously doubt if the producers of most movies and television shows know—or care—that there is a difference. Love, in its most elemental form, is desiring what is best for the object of your love. Sorry to say, in our self-obsessed, self-esteeming popular culture, wanting what is best for someone other than yourself is all too often less understood than global warming—if that's possible.

The mother in my example above wanted what was best for her son, and that would have been for him to have a happy, productive—and crime free—life. But now that he has committed the crime, what is best for him is to suffer the consequences. And she accepts that because she loves him. A newlywed husband, if pressed on the issue, would admit that what he wants for his new bride is for her to have a happy and productive life. But what he is often most obsessed with, at the moment, is the intensity of his feelings and his desire for her—the sexual attraction.

On the other hand, to like someone suggests a far less intense feeling. You may like your boss, but have no interest in a lifetime relationship (or maybe so—office romances are a subject all to themselves). It is obviously possible to like someone and not love them, and it is possible to love them and not like them. But it is difficult to stay married to someone, even though you may tell yourself that you love them, and not like them. Even more important, as Mr. Prager states, they need to become your best friend.

Some of this may seem so obvious on its face as to hardly warrant discussion. To the contrary, given our society's obsession with "love," I believe the issue of the success of a marriage being dependant on your spouse becoming your best friend is one that has been largely ignored. It is something that I implicitly felt, and it played a strong role in our marriage. Even so, it has been only in the last few years that I've had occasion to really think about the significance of the difference between liking, and loving, your wife.

Colleen and I enjoyed each other during the two years we were in junior college, from the first time we met. I think, however, that had anybody suggested to us then that we appeared to rather like each other we would have both felt a little awkward and probably embarrassed by it. We were each going steady with someone else at the time, and were together only in the context of school and studies.

We did, however, seem to keep finding ways to do that and I would sometimes badger her into having a Coke or hamburger with me when occasions permitted. We had a mutual friend who, in fact, teased us on several occasions about how much time we seemed to just happen to spend together. We would scoff at his teasing, but it merited an entry in Colleen's freshman year scrapbook a year before we had our first date. But after that first date, we quickly became best friends—well before we became husband and wife.

I found several entries in her diary to be quite prescient in this respect:

April 19,1955

Practiced Rhetoric panel with Del and the others tonight...sure was fun.

May 6, 1955

Del and I were at Masonic Temple at 8:00 AM to start on banquet decorations. Couldn't get in, so studied chemistry all day.

September 15, 1955

Del and I handed out lab supplies in chemistry for three periods, today.

September 27, 1955

...was studying chemistry...first thing I knew Del drove up...I like to kid and joke with him.

I included these examples because of what they came to mean to us later on. Neither of us suspected, at the time, that the other would have been interested in anything beyond friendship. But as we read back through those entries we were both surprised, and amused, to see how frequently I was mentioned by name when there was nothing noteworthy about what had occurred—such as handing out lab supplies together in chemistry.

I think it was that friendship that developed between us during those two years that resulted in our so quickly coming to love each other once we gave ourselves the opportunity to allow it to happen. And, I now recognize, it has been that friendship that has seen us through our difficulties and rough spots over our fifty years. Another diary entry said it even more:

April 18, 1956

Del a stranger at school again today, then came by this evening and was a swell guy again. I sure like him, after two years of curiosity.

That was written the next day after our first date. My innate shyness and insecurities had caused me to be quite distant with her the next morning, but I had gone to her house that evening and we got along fine again.

The significance of her diary entry was the comment "I sure like him, after two years of curiosity." We did, in fact, sure like each other. Two weeks after she had written that entry in her diary I shook her up by telling her I hoped to marry her—and she shook herself up even more by realizing that she was in favor of it. There is absolutely no possibility that any of that could have happened without the basis of the friendship that had grown between us during those two years.

But it's easy to be friends, or to at least be friendly, when you are first falling in love. The real role of friendship in marriage proves itself over the years that follow. As an example of what I mean by that, let me talk a little about one of my favorite things— and that's not "whiskers on kittens," it's flying.

As I mentioned in the Introduction, I'm a private pilot. I've been obsessed with planes and flying since I was in kindergarten. I don't understand it, but most people are, by and large, irrationally afraid of small planes. They think they're dangerous, and are afraid to fly in one.

But Colleen wasn't like that. She knew from the very first how much I loved planes, and always supported me. In spite of how tight money was for us then, she was as excited as I was when I took my first flying lessons while we were at Kansas State. But the money just didn't stretch far enough. It was another ten years before I was able to afford to finish getting my private pilot license and we could begin flying places together.

Colleen proved how much of a true-blue friend she really was. The wives of several of the other pilots I knew would not support their husbands at all in their love of flying. They wouldn't fly with them, and constantly complained about how unsafe it was. All those guys eventually gave it up and dropped out of flying. But for the next fifteen years, Colleen and I took our family and friends on trips all over the country. To enhance our safety, I completed training to get rated to fly only by instruments, in weather conditions that made it unsafe, and illegal, to fly by visual rules only. Colleen was never interested in learning to fly, but was always supportive through it all—a true-blue friend to this pilot.

Then one day the God of Flight smiled on me. I had the good fortune to be assigned to a group in the company at which I worked that was involved in developing a revolutionary new navigation unit for private planes. I was to be responsible for doing all the flight-testing for certification.

The first year of flight tests we flew a twin-engine plane flown by a corporate pilot. But then one day I was able to sweet-talk my boss into permitting me to use the newest, most advanced single-engine plane then available, the Piper Malibu. Because it was single-engine, I was certified to fly it myself and could thus eliminate the cost of the corporate pilot. At least, that was the argument I used on my boss.

Actually, I just lusted after that airplane. It was far faster than any I had ever flown, was pressurized, and flew at altitudes normally used by commercial aircraft. Its instrument panel looked like that of a jet airliner, and the plane placed demands on the pilot far beyond any I had ever experienced. Needless to say, I was ecstatic over the chance to get to fly it.

In due course I was ready to take off on my first trip as pilot-in-command of this sophisticated craft. It was to be a week-long trip to the west coast that required landing at some of the nation's busiest airports and flying in flight regimes that were quite new to me. I was excited, but also rather nervous. Colleen kissed me goodbye, we both wished aloud that she could be going with me, and I cranked up and headed west.

Three days later I had met numerous flight challenges, including instrument approaches into busy commercial airports. I had handled it all quite well and was gaining confidence in my abilities as a pilot. I was elated, but also feeling rather emotionally drained by the end of that third day. I had just landed at one of the busiest airports in California. After getting the plane secured and checking into a nearby hotel, I was lying on the bed in my room, winding down a bit while waiting time to go to dinner. I decided to do some journaling to record the experiences.

After relating all that had happened over the previous three days, the flight challenges and how I felt about dealing with them,

I made a concluding entry:

> I wish Colleen could have been with me on this
> trip. It would have made it all a lot more fun.

Given my obsession with flying, and the excitement of flying
an airplane that challenged me as I had never before experienced,
I should have been feeling on top of the world that evening. But
in fact, I was lonely and feeling depressed. It was four days before
our anniversary and this would be the first time we had not been
together to celebrate an anniversary.

That's what friendship in marriage is all about. I was so
accustomed to sharing everything in my life with Colleen that the
pleasure and excitement of the flying was substantially dampened
by her not being with me to share it.

That has never changed over all our years together. Regardless
of what else was going on in our lives, or the level of trouble or
stress that we were having to contend with, we liked to be together.
We like to talk to each other. Colleen is an inveterate clipper of
articles on every imaginable topic, and likes to share them with
me. She reads to me when we travel. And after fifty years of being
together, I still prefer to be alone with her than to be out mixing it
up with other people in some social situation.

I have come to the conclusion that liking the person you
marry, being best friends, is indeed one of the absolute essential
elements of a successful marriage. It is also one of marriage's
greatest rewards. You can tell yourself that you love somebody,
if for no other reason than that you are supposed to—such as
your dear old Aunt Nettie, who your parents expected you to love
because she was your blood kin. But you can't kid yourself about
liking someone. Either you do, or you don't. And if you don't like
the person you're considering spending your life with, sooner or
later it will be painfully evident and become problematic.

Of course there are other important considerations to having
a good marriage. However, before you marry, if you find yourself
preferring to be with other people, if you are excited about the

sexual attraction and involvement but don't really enjoy her company, you have a real problem—or you will have, eventually.

I've tried to analyze (I do that a lot) what it is about marriage that I have found the most rewarding. Raising a family together was certainly at the top of the list. Creating a life together, creating a home for our family, also rank high, of course. But in those early morning hours, long before sunrise when it is dark and quiet and I sit in my recliner and do all my ruminating and writing, I have to recognize that what I have most appreciated about our fifty years of marriage is our friendship—the pleasure of her company.

There is much about marriage that is quite simply utilitarian. Five thousand years of civilization have proved, contrary to all the negativity expressed today, that society functions best when founded on the nuclear family, a husband and wife working as a team to assist each other through the difficulties of life and joining to continue the species. We humans are not designed to be alone. We need emotional support and we often need physical assistance. As we age we need that even more.

Marriage is the most practical means of providing for those needs. Medical and psychological studies all affirm that for society in general married people make more money, live longer, are healthier and are less depressed than unmarried people. Being married has economic benefits, and is a health benefit right alongside a healthy diet and exercise. So even if our culture were like some, and the marriage were arranged by one's parents, it could nevertheless be a very beneficial way to live one's life.

But it would not necessarily be the most enjoyable. The practical, utilitarian advantages of a marriage are conceivably reason enough to be willing to get married, and stay married, throughout one's life. To be able to spend those years also enjoying that person—liking them—is indeed a special blessing.

I recognize thus far I've been offering rather general statements about liking your marriage partner. It would not surprise me if you thought I could be a tad more specific, say, offer some "do's and don'ts" as examples of what I mean. You might be wondering, for instance:

"If I want to watch my alma mater whip up on our hated rival Saturday afternoon, rather than going shopping for a new living room settee, is that supposed to mean I don't like my wife?"

or,

"My fiancé wants me to go with him to help pick out new golf clubs. Frankly, I hate golf. I would prefer that he go alone, and let me shop. Are you telling me that means I don't like my fiancé?"

Please. Give me a break. You don't need me to tell you the answers to questions like those. The answers depend on why you do, or do not, want to do something with your mate—and how they feel about it. It also involves that four-letter word, "fair." I write at length about fairness in a later chapter, but answers to questions like those above ultimately come down to both of you being fair.

But the point remains: you need to ask yourself whether you don't want to do those things because you want to watch the big game, or because you, in fact, wouldn't enjoy her company while you are doing it. If you like each other, if you enjoy each other's company, that oftentimes will outweigh the lack of enthusiasm you might otherwise feel about what the two of you are doing, or the enjoyment you might have missed from not getting to watch a football game on TV (Besides, that's why TIVO was invented).

Consider a couple of personal examples. The first comes from an entry in Colleen's diary:

January 5, 1957

...went into town to exchange some of our casseroles. More fun! We had a ball.

The second is from a journal entry I made, just six months shy of fifty years later:

June 30, 2006

...ran some errands coming home. I used to get so impatient when we had to do that. Colleen examines and searches a store the way an archeologist examines and searches a newly-opened Egyptian tomb, and it tends to make me break out in a rash. But I am able to handle it a lot better, now.

In the first example, it was just three weeks before our wedding, and the day after my home church had given us a shower. All the ladies of the church knew how much we would need kitchen utensils, and had greatly diminished the local inventory of casserole dishes on our behalf. We went in to my hometown the next day to exchange some of them for something a little more sophisticated—such as a skillet, or toaster. As Colleen wrote in her diary, we had a ball making those exchanges together. But we were giddy in love and would have had fun licking stamps, as long as we were together while doing it.

The second example is more to the heart of it. I hate to shop, and Colleen lives for it. She enters a state approaching beta-wave bliss when able to spend hours browsing a clothing store, or dollar-discount store—and I would almost rather have my toenails pulled out than to do so. That didn't mean I didn't like Colleen—it meant I didn't like shopping.

By the same token, Colleen didn't have any particular interest in dawdling along a flight line under a broiling sun, while I swooned over the P-51 fighters and B-17 bombers parked there for an air show. Nevertheless, she has done so, many times, because she knows how much it means to me.

But there is always that annoying little word, "fairness." So I tried to find ways to support her shopping desires, because I knew how much it meant to her. Usually, I agreed to stay home and keep the kids so she could shop without having to deal with them. Other times, she really wanted me to go with her, so I did—and some of those times I was pretty decent about it, too.

In the final analysis, Colleen and I prefer doing things together over doing them separately. We liked—and like—to be together.

And that is the key. If you like each other, and enjoy each other's company, you will find ways to do so while still recognizing that you aren't going to want to do every single thing together every single time. But it does mean that you are going to have to respect each other and find ways to be fair about the differences. I'm assuming that you know each other well enough to figure out the details for yourselves.

So there it is: you better like first, then let love come. And if you like each other, love will follow, if it is going to. I've tried various ways to differentiate them, but I'll offer these final examples of what I've been attempting to say:

- Like: what you feel as you drive across the barren plains of West Texas, working on *The New York Times* crossword puzzle together to kill time.

- Love: What you feel when you look at your wedding pictures from fifty years earlier.

- Like: What you feel while you clean up the kitchen together, cracking jokes and visiting about the evening of having friends and family for dinner.

- Love: What you feel while waiting together in the doctor's office to get test results on a debilitating disease.

Those two feelings, like and love, are all wrapped up together when it comes to a relationship, and marriage. In some ways they seem indistinguishable, but they are different. I'll conclude this with lyrics from an old Don William's song:

You placed gold on my finger
You brought love like I've never known
You gave life to our children
And to me a reason to go on

You're my bread when I'm hungry
You're my shelter from troubled winds
You're my anchor in life's ocean
But most of all, you're my best friend.

I may be exaggerating, making too much of this point. But I don't think so. I have learned, over my years, that more than anything else a good marriage is a life-long friendship. I was originally attracted to Colleen for all the usual reasons, physical and emotional. In retrospect, I have come to recognize that chief among them was the simple fact that I just liked to be with her. That's never changed. She was, is and always will be my best friend. And I know she feels the same about me. No marriage can fail when a couple can say that about themselves.

If country music and a syndicated marriage counselor agree on the point, it must be right: if you want to make a go of a lifetime together, become best friends.

Chapter 6

Getting to Know You

There is a song, written by Oscar Hammerstein II for the 1956 musical "The King and I," in which the character Anna sings to the children of the King of Siam:

> Getting to know you,
> Getting to know all about you,
> Getting to like you,
> Getting to hope you like me....

In this simple, but delightful, little song, Anna, the English schoolteacher to the King's children, touches on one of the more important prerequisites to a successful marriage. That wasn't the point of the song in the musical, but a couple considering marriage is taking a real risk if they ignore the message in the song.

It was a little difficult trying to decide whether this chapter should come first, or if the chapter on liking your mate should be first. It is rather hard to learn to like someone before you get to know them, and you won't bother to get to know them if you don't like them. The point of both chapters is simply this: for your marriage to be able to endure and be a rewarding one for both of you, it is essential that you like each other. And you won't know if you're going to like each other until, and unless, you get to know each other. And, if asked what you really know about the object of your affection, "We're in love, and that's all we need to know," is not the right answer.

Why is that, you may ask? The short answer, of course, is that before making a decision that will affect the rest of both your lives, you should know to whom it is that you are committing your life. No matter how well you may think you know each other after a few dates, or even a few months, you really don't. The reason for that, of course, is that each of us is, in reality, two people. We are the outer person that we allow others to see, the one that everyone experiences in our daily lives. But we are also the inner person, that we may or may not allow anyone else to know. How many times have you heard comments like these:

> "I don't understand it. He was so nice to me before we got married, and now he just ignores me, like he can't stand me."

Or,

> "I wish I'd known she had such a temper before we got married. Seems like she blows up at everything I do."

It is that inner person, that private person, who will in all probability have a greater influence on the success or failure of the marriage than the public one will ever have. If a marriage is to succeed and prosper, if many of the emotional minefields which can destroy both the marriage partners and the marriage itself are to be avoided, it is mandatory that the marriage partners work hard at "getting to know you, getting to know all about you"—and the sooner the better.

This issue, not knowing well enough the real personality of the person we married, certainly affected Colleen and me in our early years of marriage. Had we both better understood what was really behind the things that we said and did to cause a problem for each other, much of it could have been avoided—or at least could have been dealt with better.

Had someone asked us, shortly before we got married, how well we really knew each other I imagine we both would have insisted that we knew each other quite well. We spent considerable time together during those first two years of college. And while we were dating we spent many hours talking into the wee hours of the morning about everything from religion to where we would like to live. Colleen's diary entries from that time make frequent mention of how we "talked and talked and talked," or how we had "heart-to-heart" talks. We talked to each other all the time. (Well, not <u>all</u> the time. We were nineteen, and falling in love.)

It felt to us both that we were amazingly compatible on virtually every issue. And in most respects, we were. But there were some clues to aspects of our personalities that we glossed over, simply because we were too much in love, and too naive, to pay any attention to them. And, I suspect, we were not unusual in that respect. To illustrate what I mean, I've extracted portions of several diary entries from our early times together, that suggested a pattern.

April 17,1956

I would never have believed this Del was behind all that sarcasm....

April 18, 1956

Del was a stranger again at school, but came by tonight and was a swell guy again....

May 4, 1956

Del was a true-blue boy friend today—none of this "I guess I know you" stuff.

May15,1956

...And Del has stepped in just all of a wonderful sudden. And he's a Del I never suspected existed....

June 20,1956

Got a swell letter from Del, and he's finally sure of us....

July 20, 1956

*Del and I went out and parked. Didn't seem to hit it off too well.
He's so unsure of himself, where I'm concerned. Won't let himself
believe that I love him so much.*

We had at this point known each other for nearly two years.
We had been in several classes together, studied together, worked
together for long hours. We had dated and fallen in love. Why would
it be, then, that the person Colleen was coming to love was one she
"never suspected existed?" Why did she not expect the person "that
was behind all that sarcasm?"

Another element that played a role in all this was the insecurity
I felt regarding how Colleen felt about the guy she had been going
with for the previous six years. It took her a while, obviously, to
become confident that she was doing the right thing in leaving him
for me. But Colleen has always been able to be more secure in those
sorts of things than I ever have. Once she decided for herself that
I was the one she wanted to spend her life with, that was that. No
second thoughts.

I, on the other hand, was as firm as slab of Jello. She would tell
me that he was no longer a part of her life, and I would believe her.
I would tell her that I was finally confident of her, and her feelings
for me—then a month later we don't "hit it off" because I'm so
unsure of myself, where's she's concerned. These contradictions
played a role in our interaction with each other for far too long.

It took me marital eons to reach a point where I no longer
lived with a latent fear that she would wake up some morning
and decide that she had made a grievous mistake—and the house
would be vacant when I got home from work. It required a lot of
Colleen to avoid letting my lack of confidence not make her upset
with me. It seemed to suggest a lack of trust in her, and would
sometimes hurt her.

For the two years we were at JuCo, before we dated, Colleen
saw one kind of person. I was valedictorian of my high school,
and played on the football team. I was an A student in her classes,

president of the freshman class, then was elected Student Council president in our sophomore year. I played saxophone in the JuCo dance band. I was congenial, friendly, had a keen sense of humor and was fun to be with. I seemed confident and self-assured, sometimes to the point of being "cocky." She had noted that my "keen" sense of humor would sometimes border on being too sharp and cutting. I intended it as good-natured teasing, but she once referred to it as "sarcasm." I preferred to think of it as "incisive wit," in the Oscar Levant tradition, but I guess Colleen sometimes felt otherwise.

Up until the night of our first date, that was essentially all Colleen knew about me. She had no idea whatsoever how I felt about her, or if I felt anything at all. We obviously enjoyed each other's company, and were frequently together. But she had no way of knowing what to expect of me, or from me, that first night we went together. She had written in her diary, before our first date, wondering if I would like her well enough to even ask for a second date. What she did not expect was for me to be so strongly attracted to her. Obviously, there was more to me than I had allowed to be seen in public.

I'm going through all this for a couple of reasons. The first is to emphasize my contention that it is not all that easy to get to know that "real person" we are going to marry, or are married to. The second reason is to illustrate why I believe that is true. It is difficult because most of us, and especially us guys, are not predisposed to letting people get to know what our "real self" is; and sometimes I'm not so sure we even know ourselves.

I strongly suspect that what I experienced is not that different from what many guys experience. We have a perception of the type of person we are expected to be, or perhaps what we think we want ourselves to be, and we attempt to portray that personality to those around us. In truth, we're oftentimes not really like that. But, being guys, we keep it to ourselves. Unfortunately, that puts us in conflict with ourselves. This conflict can, and sooner or later will, affect our relationships and marriages. It is a conflict with which I have long been acquainted.

I have been aware most of my adult life that I have two conflicting personalities trying to occupy the same body. I suspect that is true, to a greater or lesser degree, for most of us and is a result of the "nature versus nurture" issue. That is, we are the person we are born to be, created by our genes and DNA. But we are also the person created by the environment in which we are raised, by the culture that surrounds us and by the expectations of those who raise us. Those two personalities can quite often be at cross purposes within us, and can cause conflicts with those close to us—such as your spouse.

Let me illustrate what I mean, and the effect it can have on a marriage, with my own experience. First, there is the way you're raised, or nurtured. I was born in the middle of the Depression, and grew up in a rural farming community. When I was five, America was plunged into World War II by the attack on Pearl Harbor. At age nine, my parents moved us to a small farm near my hometown in eastern Kansas. My grade school through junior college years were spent working on the farm.

Being a farmer in the 1930's and 1940's was a difficult and often emotionally draining way of trying to keep body and soul together. Although most farmers by the 1940s had tractors, many still used draft horses. There was an unending need for hard, physical work. It was often hot, dry and dusty. When it wasn't, the ground was either muddy or frozen solid. This was not an environment that nurtured poets and dreamers. The men of that era and locale were, for the most part, hardened, hard working, honest, taciturn, inarticulate, intensely private and undemonstrative. Most of them were good-hearted and cared for their wives and families, but the culture did not allow for the sharing and expressing of emotions. It was this stereotype of what it meant to be a man that surrounded me at all turns, and affected everything about me.

I liked to go to movies while I was growing up. I went every chance I could get. During the war years, and for several years thereafter, two types of movies frequented the theaters in my home town: westerns, starring a long list of manly heroes—John

Wayne, Gary Cooper, Gregory Peck, Randolph Scott, and a host of others—and war movies, usually starring the same names. In either genre, men were quiet, not-to-be-messed-with types that always got the job done. In the background, there was always the good-looking, patiently-waiting love interest.

They would look at each other, unspeaking, as he was about to walk out the door to fight either cattle rustlers or enemy soldiers. In either case, we knew he would (a) win, and (b) be back someday to his love. But we also knew that we would never hear him tell her that he loved her, or see him kiss her. We just knew it was true. We didn't have to see it. If you want to get the "Cliff Notes" version of what men were like, and were expected to be like, during those years, just watch Gary Cooper in *High Noon* and John Wayne in *The Searchers*.

I make no attempt to hide the fact that I liked those "real men." I liked trying to be one. I have a picture, taken the summer after I graduated from high school, of me driving an old truck. I worked for a farm neighbor that summer, driving his truck for farm work. It was an old, beat-up Chevy with a large dump box-bed. That truck was the very definition of a man's truck—all manual, with no power anything, and no discernible creature comforts.

As was typical then of how things were done, I was given no instructions or guidance on how to drive it. I was just told to take it to the field and drive along side the field chopper, about four feet away from it, while it chopped the rows of corn and blew them into the truck bed. As I left the farmer's house that first morning, and tried to shift into fourth gear, all I got was a horrid grinding sound of gears stripping and refusing to mesh.

But I had just turned eighteen, and considered myself to be an expert driver. No broken down piece of General Motors was going to best me. I had frequently heard the men-folk talk of having to "double-clutch," but wasn't certain I knew what that meant or how to do it. This seemed like the time to find out if it worked. So I quickly pushed in the clutch, shifted into neutral, released the clutch, revved up the engine, pushed in the clutch again—and slipped into fourth gear, as slick as a whistle. My heart nearly burst with the pride of accomplishment. Real men knew how to double-clutch.

There is an aspect of being a male that relishes being able to overcome physical obstacles, to meet the challenges of the physical world. I'll be quite honest: Some of my most exhilarating, and for that matter memorable, moments have come when I was challenged by—and threatened by—some physical experience, met the challenge and lived to tell about it. I've never had to be in combat, so have to take on face value the words of Winston Churchill, who once said, "There is nothing more exhilarating than being shot at without result." I am well enough aware, now, of what actual combat must be like, and what it does to a person who experiences it, to know that Churchill's comments had to be a bit facetious.

In no way have I ever experienced anything like combat, and don't mean to compare my experiences to those who have. Nevertheless, I have had some close calls while driving tractors, on runaway horses, and involving in-flight emergencies that could easily have resulted in serious injury or death. I never openly admitted it, but those experiences, once survived, were in a very real sense some of the most thrilling moments of my life. That element of being male, of being exhilarated by "being shot at without result," is as real as the hair on our chests (if we have any).

Thus it was, as I grew up, that I was attracted to the look of John Wayne as he searched for the Indians who had massacred the family that he loved, or of Gary Cooper walking alone down the street at high noon, about to face the men who wanted to kill him. They were "men's men" and never backed away from trouble, or duty. They defended hearth and home, believed in "Duty, Honor, Country" and never ran from responsibility—but kept their mouths shut about it. I admired those traits, and wanted to be like those men. And in most ways, I still do. I think there is much to be admired about them.

Because those men were my role models while I was growing up, it is no wonder that I appeared to be self-assured when Colleen first came to know me. That's the way real men were, the way I wanted to be, and the way I made myself appear to be whenever in public. But, as Paul Harvey would say, "Now you get to hear the rest of the story."

As much as I wanted to be like the "real men" described above, I was in many ways completely unlike them. This is the "nature" side of the personality issue. As much as I wanted to be like Gary Cooper, I was in many respects more like my favorite uncle, who was the antithesis of all that I described above. He was a quiet, studious, passive and gentle man with a wry sense of humor, who made his career in journalism. I also greatly admired my chemistry teacher in high school (the same one Colleen and I had in JuCo). He influenced Colleen and me in many ways during our school years, and for many years thereafter.

That outer self—confident, self assured, good-natured— was the only side of me that Colleen had been allowed to see before we started dating. But I was also my inner self— quiet, studious, diffident, shy, moody, unsure of myself in any relationship. What you see is not always what you get. Those hidden facets of my personality fairly quickly began to make their appearance as Colleen and I began falling for each other. As soon as I began to be aware of how strongly I felt about her, my insecurities started surfacing.

Colleen also had two facets to her personality—ones that took me years to fully recognize and accept. When we first began to get to know each other she appeared to be a lot like me. She always seemed friendly and congenial. She was rarely seen, at least when not concentrating on studies or class work, without her beaming, trademark smile. But she was also determined to excel, and strong-willed. She always appeared to be the epitome of self-confidence, able to take on any task and excel at it. And she drove herself mercilessly in her determination to get an A in every class she took.

But, like each of us, Colleen was influenced by her environment and upbringing. As I said earlier, the Depression made life a hard-scrabble battle for farmers, and Colleen's family was not untouched by that. She grew up not being a stranger to having to "make-do." She also, because of the isolation of their farm, had little opportunity to socialize with kids her age. Thus, even though her high school was small by any standard, she had to learn to adapt herself to the new environment, and to the "town kids" who seemed to her to be so much more worldly than she felt she was.

Her isolated childhood had made her shy and hesitant around others. This hesitancy led to her being considered by certain classmates to be "stuck-up," she learned one day when a boy in her class made a very public criticism of her. Rather than being offended by this accusation, and going off in a snit, she merely decided she was not going to let it persist and made a determined effort to become more overtly friendly. That was her nature. If she saw something that needed fixing, she tried to fix it.

It was this friendly, out-going version of herself that I came to know in JuCo, just as it was that version of me that she came to know. It's not that it was superficial, or hypocritical, for either one of us. We were, in fact, friendly, confident people. But we were also both inwardly shy and self-conscious. We were just determined to not let it deter us. So, the Colleen I knew when we met and fell in love, and the Colleen that I thought I had married, was a person who was not just friendly and out-going, but who was also supremely capable, self-confident and self-assured—my own personal copy of "Wonder Woman."

What I came to understand about her, eventually, was that she was in fact very security-conscious, to the point of being fearful of change. She wanted her status to remain quo—and orderly. She wanted her life to be predictable, and to follow the outline that she had so carefully created for it. That last month of JuCo, in which she left her boyfriend of six years, accepted that she and I would get married, and decided to go with me to Kansas State instead of the teacher's college she had planned on attending, shook her up in ways I didn't comprehend for many years.

She masqueraded that fear very well, as years went by, agreeing to any change in locale or lifestyle that I suggested as I moved along in my efforts to get my Master's Degree and to start my career. She supported me in every way, without any apparent hesitation or problem. We would not have made some of the life choices we made, had she not done so. What I did not know, at least directly, was how much she feared most of those changes. But it was always there beneath the surface, and caused stress and worry that manifested itself in unrelated ways, sometimes leading to upset feelings between us. It took me a long time to recognize and understand what was at the root of it all.

So what we both had to come to understand was that each of us was the person we had come to know and like and love at JuCo, but we were also complicated, multi-faceted people with personality traits that caused us both to have problems and hurt each other's feelings. Because we liked each other, and loved each other, we never let those problems and hurt feelings persist, or seriously affect our marriage. But too often, now, such problems do result in a broken marriage and disrupted lives.

I know that what was true for us is true for many people. We don't know each other very well when we get married, and the things we learn after the fact can become problematic. In certain respects, that is unavoidable. It takes time to get to know a person, and most of us don't want to wait to get married. But we can at least be better prepared. "Forewarned is forearmed" is good advice not just for the commanding officer of an army, but for a couple planning on marriage, as well. Knowing that there are going to be "surprises" about your partner will at least let you be prepared for them, and not be blind-sided by them.

There are many ways to do this. In Chapter 12, I mention my belief that a couple should seek counseling prior to marriage (I also make the point that I prefer to think of it as marriage "training," instead of counseling). Most marriage counselors (trainers?) have all sorts of things in their bags of tricks to help a couple uncover any surprises that may be in store for them in their mate-to-be. They are also trained at helping the couple learn to cope with them before they create problems.

Colleen gave me a birthday card recently that included a line in its verse that speaks to my point:

> I know I have someone who understands the parts
> of me that other people don't even know exist.

That's what I mean by "getting to know you," and what marriage is all about. At first, it's about getting to know each other well enough to know how to interact, how to get along day in and day out. But as time goes by, and that becomes more second nature, it's about getting to know the very core of each other, to "understand the parts that other people don't even know exist." And to make a point that I attempt to make throughout this book, that isn't going to happen until, and unless, you commit your lives to each other and stay married long enough that it can happen.

I strongly suggest, recommend, urge, stress that whether you are already married, or only planning to be, that you both make every effort to learn to better know each other. There are too many sources of support available today to aid you in that effort to be able to justify not doing so. As you do so, you are each going to learn things about the other that may be a surprise, or even a bit of a shock. You may be pleasantly surprised to learn how deeply your mate truly feels about you. It may also uncover some elements of your personalities that are problematic and the potential source of future trouble. The sooner you are aware of all those elements and facets of each other, the sooner you can start the process of learning to understand them and deal with them. Perhaps, then, you can reminisce about them, many years later as you prepare for your golden anniversary celebration.

Chapter 7

Respect

In the previous chapters, I have discussed at length two factors that I believe are of fundamental importance to the success of any marriage: getting to know your partner, and becoming best friends. There is a third factor that I consider to be of equal importance: respecting the person you are going to marry. I would go so far as to suggest that to marry a person you know you don't respect is to be more unfair to them than if you stood them up at the altar.

"Respect" is a word we often use, but probably just as often give little thought as to what we really mean by it. I would also suspect that the nuances of its meaning often are overlooked. We respect the office of the President of the United States (or at least we do when we approve of its current occupant), we respect our parents, we respect our elders (at least we used to). Again referring to my Random House dictionary, we find the following meanings for the word "respect":

1. A feeling of appreciative, often deferential regard; esteem.
2. The state of being regarded with honor or esteem.
3. Willingness to show consideration or appreciation.

I mentioned earlier, in relating the Academy Award speech by Sally Field, that her first concern was that her peers respect her. We all want respect. Tragic numbers of teenagers have been killed by some brainless gang member who believed that the—now dead—offender had "dissed" him. To translate, he had "disrespected" the "offendee." Apparently, being respected is worthy of committing murder to correct its perceived absence, at least in their dysfunctional universe.

I doubt that anyone would suggest that respect should not be part of a marriage, but what does it really mean in terms of how we interact with our spouse? I imagine that it is somewhat like the quote attributed to the late Supreme Court Justice Potter Stewart, in his concurrence on an obscenity case. Pornography may be hard to define, he wrote, but "I know it when I see it." I believe respect is like that. Or, if I may state it in the negative, we know what disrespect is when we see it. And no marriage can long survive consistent disrespect of one spouse by the other.

I further believe that respect—or the lack of it—serves as the basis for all the other aspects of how we treat each other. Chances are we will not be too inclined to like a person, to be fair, considerate and polite to a person, for whom we have no respect.

But what do I mean by the word?

I believe that I would have to go with a short version of definition number two: the state of being regarded with esteem. Of course, when you look up the definition of esteem it gets a bit cyclical. To hold someone in high esteem is defined, at least in part, as respecting them. But it also means to appreciate, or place a high value on. I like that definition. If a husband doesn't esteem, doesn't appreciate, his wife and place a high value on her, there's going to be "trouble in River City." Of course, that works in reverse, too. A wife must just as surely respect her husband.

This wasn't included in the definitions given above, but I also believe that to respect someone means that you consider them to be your equal, if not your superior. And, I suppose, that's what I am really getting at when I state that respect is of fundamental importance to a marriage. You're not likely to treat in some demeaning, condescending fashion a person that you consider to be equal, or even superior in some sense of the word, to yourself. And conversely, it's hard to avoid being condescending and patronizing to someone who you feel is inferior to you.

So what does it mean, in terms of day-to-day living, to respect your spouse? Most husbands and or wives would, in all probability, claim that, "of course I respect my wife/husband." But what Colleen and I all too often witness are examples to the contrary.

For instance, Colleen and I are both disturbed by how frequently we see a husband (yes, guys, wives do it to us, too) do something to his wife that leaves us just shaking our heads, wondering aloud, "how can he have so little respect for someone he presumably loves?" Maybe it is something so simple and innocuous as walking on into the restaurant ahead of her, leaving her to trail along across the parking lot behind him—which we have, in fact, seen occur several times.

Another such example of disrespect—and a pet peeve for Colleen and me—is criticizing your spouse, and especially doing so in public. We are both appalled when we hear a husband or wife tear down their mate in front of others. We agreed early in our marriage that we would never do that, and never have. If we have a disagreement over something when we are out and about, or visiting friends, we don't share it, or air it, until we are alone.

That's not the only example of disrespect. We have all heard comments made by married couples, such as:

> "Mabel is a lousy cook—doesn't seem like her
> mother taught her a thing, in the kitchen."

Or similarly,

> "George is so lazy around the house—just won't
> help with anything I have to do."

Such accusations may be factual, and may make the person feel better for the moment when venting them, but they are corrosive in their effect on a relationship and marriage. They eat away at it, and damage the marriage and relationship in ways that are often irretrievable and irreparable. Each such comment, in and of itself, may not be of much significance. But it does two things, and both are bad.

First, it is a demeaning humiliation of your spouse. Even if it is only a small one, and even if stated more or less in private, it is still destructive. And there's nothing good that can come of that. Second, it is like whacking away at a tree with a small hatchet. No single blow is going to fell the tree, but it can weaken it to the point that a major blow—or blow-up, as in an argument—can topple it. And there's nothing good that can come of that, either. Unless, of course, it is to finally be free of incessant criticism.

On the other hand, respecting your spouse often manifests itself in many little ways. On the surface, many of these may hardly seem worth mentioning. Picking up your own dirty clothes, carrying your own dirty dishes—and hers, while you're at it—to the kitchen when the meal is finished, saying "excuse me" when you inadvertently interrupt, offering to bathe the kids when you know she is tired from a long day, just as tired as you are. It could be agued that such things are simply "being nice." And that's correct. But, I maintain, it's very difficult to be nice to someone for whom you have no respect. You do nice things because you respect your mate, and could not feel right about doing otherwise.

As another example of showing—or, more accurately, not showing—respect, I'll relate a little story about Colleen's dad that always sort of bothered both of us. It was a trivial thing, in the grand scheme of life, but said a lot about marriage relationships. The lavatory in the bathroom at her home was one of the old style that had a rubber stopper for the drain, rather than having the push-rod that is now standard. Usually, such a stopper was connected to the faucet by a small chain, so that the stopper could be pulled to drain the lavatory without having to reach into the dirty water to get it. The problem was that, in this case, there was no chain.

Many times, when we were visiting her folks, her dad, Claude, would have shaved and left the stopper in the lavatory, submerged under a basin full of lathery, whiskery water. He obviously found it not to his liking to reach in and unplug it. So he left it for someone else to do. Why he didn't just buy a chain to put on it, I don't know. Of course, I guess I could have done it for him, but I didn't. I'm not sure why, as I think back on it.

Now keep in mind that Claude adored his only daughter, and Colleen felt much the same toward him. He and I also got along well. Colleen was amazed at how quickly and easily he and I became friends after Colleen and I started dating, and at how well we got along together. It surprised, and pleased her so much, because in the six years she went with her former boyfriend, Claude had never warmed up to him. We have countless pictures of Claude and me sitting at a table somewhere, sharing a cup of coffee and yet another tall tale of some sort. We enjoyed driving around the countryside, just looking things over and visiting, or stopping for coffee and pie at some hamburger joint. I knew he respected me, as I did him, and over the years he became what I considered to be my closest friend—after Colleen, of course.

Thus, it was perplexing to both Colleen and me that he would leave such an unpleasant little task, one that was clearly his responsibility, for one of us to have to do. It didn't seem like him. Yet, we both implicitly knew that it was the result of nothing more or less than habit. He was quite accustomed to leaving that unpleasant task to his wife, and probably never gave it a moment's thought.

I doubt that it ever occurred to him that we might be the ones stuck with having to clean up his mess, or how we might perceive it. I imagine that it would have embarrassed him, had he realized that it bothered us. But it obviously didn't bother him that his wife had to do it. It was a small thing, yet said much about the concept of respect—or the lack of it—of a husband for a wife. Unfortunately, that lack of respect took a toll on their marriage, over the years.

Respect is manifested in big ways, too. One of the things that I feel best about from my own perspective has to do with Colleen finishing college. I tried to make it clear in our "Sixteen Days" story how determined Colleen was to get a college degree. It was more than simply a desire, or something she believed she needed for a sense of financial security. She had predicated her whole life plan, her perception of who and what she wanted to be, on having a degree in homemaking. In many ways, it was to define her as a person.

That determination would not allow her to compromise and attend the college her boyfriend of several years was attending, because it didn't have an adequate Home Economics department. The resultant separation was a major factor in contributing to them breaking up, and in making it possible for us to start going together. It literally changed our lives.

Her determination to get her degree, and to excel while doing it, caused her to be fearful of getting married while in college. She rightly recognized the demands that it would place on her, and how divided her time and loyalties would become. She wouldn't even consider it with him, and was apprehensive about it for us. Problem was, we really didn't want to wait two years to get married. Our first summer together we talked it through and decided we would get married the following summer—we would then have only one year of college to finish, and thought we could make that work.

But fate always has a way of snookering our plans. That first semester, she was staying in one of the women's dormitories (no, they were decidedly not co-ed), and I was in a boarding house off campus. Shortly after we started classes, the owners of the boarding house were ordered to cease boarding students. It wasn't really a boarding house, but a residence in a typical neighborhood of middle-class homes. The owners were a retired couple trying to make a few extra bucks to help them meet their expenses. Apparently their neighbors felt that stashing a few college students in the basement lowered the property values of the neighborhood. I was told I would have to move at the end the term.

I still remember the event quite clearly. Colleen and I were walking across campus that day, and I told her the news. My solution to my problem was to suggest what I thought was the most logical and sensible thing that we could do—that we go ahead and get married.

We had already agreed we would get married the following summer. It just seemed to make sense in the face of this unexpected need to move that we not put it off until then. What would be the point of waiting? I presumed we could get married over Christmas break.

Being a male, and having given it not a whole lot of thought, I assumed that Colleen would enthusiastically jump at the suggestion. Her apparent hesitation and lack of enthusiasm for my suggestion threw me a curve, and caused me to temporarily get my nose out of joint. Her diary entries from that time, which I didn't read until many years later, painted a very different picture.

October 3, 1956

...he wants to get married. I'm afraid I want too badly to have a wedding that's not squeezed between Xmas and New Years to do it. I'm all confused and befuddled.

October 4,1956

I'm all confused and scared. The question of whether to get married Xmas is real, and not imaginary any more. I know how Del feels now, and that's real, too—more real than any of the things I've been worrying about. I want him, and need him, and he needs me just as much, or more. Dear God, what is the answer?

I had no idea, at the time, that she was going through such agonizing—she kept it pretty much to herself. But what I interpreted as a lack of enthusiasm over getting married was just her fear and concern about the limited time available for a wedding. She had a far more realistic awareness than I did of all that would be required to be ready for a wedding. She did not want the most special day in her life to be crammed in between a final exam and decorating the Christmas tree. I was simply too dense to recognize what was really behind her hesitation.

Her diary entry the next day was a much happier one. We got it all talked through, and decided to go ahead and get married, but during the semester break at the end of January. We would have more time to prepare for it, and there would not be all the holiday complications.

Lurking beneath all her initial hesitancy was her dream of getting her degree. Her marriage, and her degree, were the two most important aspects of her life and she didn't want to short-change either one. She had feared from her first day at JuCo that she would never be able to handle both. She, far more than I, recognized all that would be imposed on her and our relationship, on top of the stress of classes. She was quite prescient in her apprehensions. as her diary entries from our first year, or so, of marriage show:

February 28, 1957

School is getting us down. We don't have time to get our lessons with work, too. And we have to work. It's a rather vicious circle. We hurry and rush so, and the weeks speed by, leaving us spinning and worn out to start the next.

March 25, 1957

How will we ever live through this week, with no break over the weekend? Del is so tired, and is just snowed under with tests this week. Gee, I wish it was summer.

April 9, 1958

So far no job offers for summer. We're really sweating it. Don't know what on earth we're going to do…

From the time we got married, until well after we had left college, her diary had recurring entries like those above. Colleen's fears about marriage and college were well-founded. It proved to be almost more than we could handle, much of the time. We had essentially no financial assistance and were stone broke most of the time. We had no alternative but to work to pay our expenses, and that took time away from studies—and from each other. We simply had no time to get used to each other, to married life, and to enjoy the experience of being newlyweds.

Some of our difficulties were self-inflicted. We were both determined to be "A" students, Colleen being even more obsessed about it than I was. We spent far more time on classes and homework than was absolutely required, but we both seemed to be genetically incapable of doing otherwise. But the pressure, and the fact that we were both dog-tired all the time, led to conflicts. I discuss it in more detail later, but we didn't always handle those conflicts as well as we could have. Nevertheless, we did see it through, and both graduated.

I relate all this to emphasize the point that no matter how difficult it was for us during college, I never once considered that Colleen should stop working on her degree and work full time to put me through. There was a common joke among married couples on campus at that time to the effect that the husband was working on a Bachelor's degree, and his wife on a PhT—"putting hubby through." Many of the married couples did just that. The wife worked full time to pay the bills, while the husband worked on a degree full time.

I wish, in retrospect, that I had handled the stress better than I did some of the time. In spite of that, I am proud that I never once considered that she had less of a right to her degree than I did to mine. In fact, I believe I am more proud of that one fact than just about anything else where our marriage is concerned. That is, not once did I feel that she should drop out and put me through. She graduated three days before our second anniversary, and I wrote on her anniversary card (yes, she kept all the cards we gave each other, so I was able to read it again, not so long ago) that I was more proud of her accomplishment than anyone else could possibly have been—and I meant every word of it. We have an old black and white photo of Colleen holding her diploma, taken just after the graduation ceremony. The smile on her face in that photo makes every thing we went through worth it.

I believe that is what respect is about. I considered Colleen to be my equal—superior, in many ways—and took it for granted that she had as much right as I did to see her dream of a degree become reality. I not only did not begrudge it, I wanted it for her as much as she did. So we respected each other, and did what we had to do to see it through.

We used to talk of putting a person on a pedestal. Societies have, for centuries, put statues on pedestals of people who had earned the respect and admiration of that society. That practice has largely been dropped from our culture in recent generations, but the expression of "putting someone on a pedestal," has hung around as an indication of how much that person is esteemed and respected. Viewing your spouse this way is a pretty good basis for a long-term relationship.

I know that such a concept gets the feminist's bloomers in a twist, nowadays. They would have us believe that to do so is an insult to a woman. Perhaps not as egregious an affront as holding a door open for them, but unacceptable, nevertheless. As evidence of that, Gloria Steinem claimed that a "pedestal is as much a prison as any small, confined space."

I understand her point, at least in a technical sense. But I nevertheless believe that a husband should always, conceptually, have his wife on a pedestal. That is, he should honor and revere her, hold her in the utmost esteem. It sounds silly, perhaps outdated, in our modern culture, where Madonna and Britney Spears serve as role models for our daughters. But I offer the following example, that I believe serves as a far better role model for a marriage.

When we first left college, we moved into a mobile home park in rural New Jersey. We soon met a retired couple at the small church we began to attend who, as luck would have it, lived just down the hill below our mobile home. They had just moved into their new retirement home, and invited us down to visit one Sunday after church. She was a silver-haired, old-school lady, graciousness incarnate, and he was a dapper, mustachioed gentleman. They had been born and raised in our home state of Kansas, so we had an immediate rapport. They were Dosie and "Pop-Pop" to their grandchildren, and so they became to us.

They did two things for Colleen and me, for which I will be eternally grateful. First, they became lifelong friends, and later the godparents of our three children. But more than that, they showed us, now in our fourth year of marriage, what a marriage should be and what the relationship between a husband and wife should be. Dosie was the epitome of charm and grace. If I ever heard her say a critical thing about anyone, it was couched in such gentle wrapping that it was too disguised for me to recognize it as such.

And, as was clear to all to see, Pop-Pop had placed his Dosie on a pedestal when they got married, and there she stayed until the day he departed to prepare their home in Heaven. They were, in every way that would have made Gloria Steinem proud, partners and equals. Never once did I see or detect any sense of Dosie feeling she had to be deferential to Pop-Pop, except in the ways that she chose to do so. But, as she once said about the relationship they established early in their marriage, "I was a kept lady." Pop-Pop honored her, revered her, but above all respected her—held her in high esteem. I never in all the many years we got to know them ever heard an unpleasant, critical or disparaging word pass between them. It's hard to imagine a marriage failing in that environment—so how is "putting your spouse on a pedestal" a bad thing?

I could go on and on about this topic, but it would soon become redundant. I would like to believe that not very many of us have any real trouble figuring out when we are treating someone disrespectfully. So it's not too likely that you need me, or anyone else, to tell you how to do it. There is a story that has stuck in my mind, since I read it years ago, and it somehow seems an appropriate one to use to conclude this chapter.

The story has nothing to do with marriage, but has everything to say about respect. It is a story included in the book *Brave Men*, by Ernie Pyle, the beloved journalist who accompanied American soldiers in many theaters during World War II. He had a way of writing about the ordinary "dogface" that was always personal, poignant and compelling. He accompanied some of the troops during the incomprehensibly rugged fighting in the mountains of Italy.

In the book, Pyle tells the story of a Captain Waskow, a company commander. He was young, only in his twenties, but had led his company from the time they had left the States. His men (mostly, they were boys, chronologically, but in every real sense of the word they were men) loved him, and would follow him anywhere. Their comments indicated how they felt about him: "He always looked after us." "I've never known him to do anything unfair." "After my father, he came next."

Each night pack mules would haul ammunition and supplies up the narrow mountain trail to the front lines, and come back down with dead soldiers strapped across them. The soldiers would be laid out at the base of the trail until they could be taken on down the mountain for burial. On this moonlit night, one of the men noticed that among the bodies was that of Captain Waskow. Ernie sensed that the men around him were beginning to move toward the form of Captain Waskow, now lying with the others on the ground. Each one would look silently at their fallen leader, then offer a quiet comment as if to say a last goodbye. Ernie was close enough he could overhear them.

"God damn it!" muttered one, and then he walked away.

"God damn it to hell!" another added. He looked for a moment, then left.

Another spoke as if the captain were still alive. "I'm sorry, old man," he said, then drifted away.

Another squatted beside him, holding the captain's hand, for several minutes. Then he laid his hand down, straightened the points on the captain's shirt collar, and arranged his tattered uniform around the wound. Then he stood up and walked down the road in the moonlight, alone.

Respect. I may not know how to define it, but I know it when I see it.

From Chapter 1, "Sixteen Days"

Colleen, 1956, while we were in Junior College. Couples can usually point to a "special moment" in their relation when they realized that they were attracted to each other. Ours happened rather quickly, the night of our first date. Can you blame me?

From Chapter 2, "Epiphany"

It was looking at this picture of our wedding early one morning that made me realize, after nearly 50 years of marriage, just how important that decision had been to me, and how much marriage had meant to me for all those years. That ultimately led to writing this book.

From Chapter 5, "Like, Then Love"

I said it in the chapter: "Marriage is a lifetime journey with your best friend." A successful marriage won't— can't—last, unless you like each other, and become best friends. I think this photo, from 1958 while we were in college at Kansas State University, shows that we did, in fact, "really like each other."

From Chapter 7, "Respect"

This smile on Colleen's face, taken minutes after she got her coveted Bachelor's degree at K-State in 1959, made everything we had to go through for her to get it worthwhile. Enduring hardships can be hard on a marriage, but respecting each other, and seeing them through together, can strengthen a marriage. And pictures like this make it worth it.

From Chapter 10, "On Being a Man"

This is White Sands Missile Range in New Mexico in 1961. It was feeling sorry for myself here, while having to be gone from Colleen for weeks to work on this missile system, that led to the infamous letter that caused me to have to apologize 45 years later to Colleen for my unfairness.

Also from "On Being a Man"

No, this isn't me. It's Gary Cooper, starring as Marshall Will Kane in the iconic movie *High Noon*. This movie strongly influenced us guys coming of age in 1952, and served to show us what being a man was all about. Of course, as I matured and came of age, I learned there is much more to being a man than just the version depicted in that movie.

More from "Like, Then Love"

Me and my "other love," the Piper Malibu that I talk about in that chapter. Colleen's respect for, and support of, my love of flying played a big role in our marriage.

1957

Married 50 minutes (probably less)

Fifty minutes to fifty years.

That's what marriage is all about: committing yourselves to each other for the remainder of your lives. Staying the course. I in no way could have anticipated, when I held my smiling new bride close for that picture to the left, what all we would experience in our journey that took us to a mountain lodge fifty years later to celebrate the experience and the accomplishment. As I say in my concluding thoughts: "If there is a better way to spend life, and to end life, I can't imagine what it could be."

2007

Married 50 years

Chapter 8

Communication

If you haven't seen Paul Newman in *Cool Hand Luke*, I would recommend you do so at your earliest convenience. Even if you haven't seen the movie, you've probably heard the famous line from it:

> "What we've got here, is a failure to communicate."

You knew it was coming. There can't be a book on marriage that does not include a chapter on communication—or the failure thereof. And because it has been so thoroughly "cussed and discussed," as my Daddy used to say, I'm not going to dwell on it too much—at least not in the usual "how-to" sense. Problem is, communication between husband and wife, male and female, is just so everlastingly complicated, confusing and downright difficult.

What *she* thinks she says is,

> "Honey, I'm tired. Would you please bathe the kids, tonight? I know you've been slaving hard all week and the football game is riveting, but I'd appreciate it ever so much and love you eternally for it."

What *he* thinks she says is,

> "You lazy, indolent bum—can't you ever in your life take the initiative to do anything to help

around here without my having to kick your lazy
butt off the couch to do it?"

Venus and Mars. What we've got here, is a failure to
communicate.

Communication, by rights, ought to have been my favorite
chapter in this treatise. My electrical engineering specialty was
in communications. Not communications in the more common
sense, as in a career in TV or radio, for example, or in the sense
of popular psychology. I mean in the sense of the design of radio
receivers and antennas and of how electromagnetic signals are
transmitted from earth to the moon, or to your cell phone.

I took courses full of gobbledy-gook equations on how to
communicate the most possible information using the least
possible energy (there's a guy kind of criterion, for you). My
Masters Degree thesis was on the fundamental limitations to
the capability of a system to receive a signal—to "hear" what is
being sent. But it has required most of my life and marriage to
truly understand what it means to communicate—and, I suspect,
Colleen would occasionally be of the opinion that I still haven't
reached that point.

You're aware, I'm sure, of the rhetorical question, "If a tree
falls in a forest and there's no one there to hear it, does it still make
a sound?" Of course, you also know the variant we guys use in a
pathetic attempt to gain sympathy: "If a guy says something in a
forest, and there's no woman there to hear it, does that mean he's
still wrong?"

The point I'm trying to "communicate" here is that there
is a world of difference between a person "hearing" the sound
that's transmitted from someone else, and of their "message"
being received.

A tragic and expensive example of such a problem was the
loss some years ago of a mission to Mars. The instructions to fire
the on-board rockets to alter the trajectory for entry into a Mars
orbit were correctly sent from the ground transmitters. The signals
were duly received by the Mars-bound unit. The transmission and

reception of the signals were essentially perfect. The only problem was that the instructions transmitted were in English dimensional units, and the on-board equipment was programmed to receive in metric units. The rocket firing was disastrously wrong, and the mission lost. Likewise, in marriage what you think you're hearing may not be what she thinks she's saying.

Given the extent to which the problem of communication, or the lack of it, between male and female has been treated by all forms of media, one could assume by now that the issue is well understood by all. Unfortunately, such is not the case. We, male and female, simply think too differently for the problem to ever vanish, even in the face of over-exposure. I saw a comic strip in our local newspaper recently that speaks to the point.

The comic strip is *Baldo.* In it, young Baldo has a job at an auto parts store, and is secretly captivated by a very cute co-worker. In a previous strip, he has complained to her about a problem they have encountered at their place of work. The conversation goes as follows:

Cute co-worker: "Look, Baldo. Stuff happens, and sometimes there's no explanation for it." Baldo looks blank, so she continues: "Maybe you can say it is somehow related to centuries of social stratification, whereby some peoples and cultures find themselves on the outside looking in, never really becoming part of the mainstream, not because they don't want to, but because they aren't allowed to."

Baldo continues to look blank. She looks at him, waiting for a response.

Cute co-worker: "Does that make sense?"

Baldo doesn't reply, but thinks: *Gosh, she's cute.*

And so it goes. What we have here is a failure to communicate. Baldo had no idea what his cute co-worker had said. He heard her words, but was receiving a message that she didn't intend to be transmitting. And he failed to even attempt to communicate to her what he was thinking. So—nothing was actually communicated at all. It is a problem that most couples have to contend with, and in many respects is one that never really goes away.

The problem of communication is quite likely different for each couple. I recognize, now, that at least to some extent the problems that Colleen and I had to work through in our earlier years—and still do, at times—can be traced to the differences in the way we attempted to communicate. As I have said before, we liked to talk to each other. We talked about everything, all the time. Yet, when a problem did arise, it was not infrequently because one of us had not understood what the other had attempted to communicate.

Our church talks about sins of omission and of commission— the things we do that we shouldn't, and the things we don't do that we should (I have joked, at times, that this would seem to say it doesn't matter if we did it, or didn't do it, it's still a sin). Our communication problems were a result of both—that is, they resulted both from what we did, and from what we did not, say to each other. Of course, they also resulted from the manner in which we did, or did not, say them. It seemed, at times, that we were each speaking a different language. Turns out, in fact, we were.

Had I not happened on to the book I mentioned earlier, *The Five Love Languages*, by Dr. Chapman, I'm not sure I would have ever fully understood just how true that was. But in his book, Dr. Chapman describes how different individuals communicate, and express their feeling and love for another—and how they sense that the other one loves them. Some do it by giving gifts or by acts of service. Others need physical contact and words of affirmation. He refers to them as the five "love languages."

There is no doubt that Colleen and I—and I would suspect it's true for most couples—express our feelings for each other differently, and need to have them shown to us differently. Even though we knew we loved each other, we were not as effective at communicating those feelings as we could have been, and should have been, some of the time. We never let the problems seriously affect our marriage, and over the years we have learned to handle them better than we used to. But I suspect that had we been better able to communicate, to speak each other's "love language," those times would have been easier for us.

I don't plan to dwell on this, so it is a rather short chapter. My principal, and perhaps only, point is that communication within your marriage will always be a possible source of problems. So consider this chapter to be a "heads up," if nothing else. I do urge both of you to make every effort to recognize the problem, before it becomes a problem. Learn to understand how each of you communicates, how you "hear" what is being said.

There are virtually unlimited resources available on this subject. Take advantage of them. Read Dr. Chapman's book. Talk about it. Get counseling if your problems of communication are serious enough. Failure to communicate can send Mars missions off into the hinterlands of space, and it can send a marriage off into the hinterlands of hurt feelings and even divorce. But it is a solvable problem, if not allowed to fester.

Chapter 9

Love Life

Forget it. I'm old-fashioned, and don't consider that our love life is anyone else's business—so you're not going to get all, or any, of the salacious details. Besides, my grandkids might read this someday, and what might they think if they knew that Granddad and Grandmom…oh well, you get the point.

I debated for quite some time about whether to include something on "that" subject. Of course, no book on marriage is considered to be complete without a chapter on sex, so I assumed I should. My primary problem is not so much that I have nothing to say, or consider that it is not important, but that what I have to say seems to be so futile. Or perhaps I should say I feel so futile in saying it, because I doubt that much of anyone would take it seriously, nowadays.

We—American society, that is—have some real problems on our hands on the issue of what used to be considered a subject too private to discuss in public, i.e., sex. What has been done by our society to what was known to my grandparents as "conjugal bliss" is inexcusable—an affront to and diminution of everything that is good about what should be the ultimate expression of love between two people. No small part, if not all, of my problem with this subject is the degree to which that expression of love has become trivialized by our popular culture, so much so that this trivialization has permeated our entire society.

What was once politely referred to as "making love" has deteriorated to "having sex." It sounds like you're ordering a steak—"I'll have the sex, very rare." Of course, that expression is quite delicate compared to what is now commonly used, that abomination of the English language, the "f-word." How can something that is referred to by such a gutter-worthy term be considered an act so private, so special, as to be worth waiting until marriage to experience, or worth "saving yourself" for? Shopping at K-Mart would seem to be held in higher esteem.

I know I'm on a soapbox here, but frankly, it really gets to me. I liked the atmosphere of romance, mystery and magic that was a part of that more "innocent" time. I'm glad that I came of age and fell in love in the 1950s and got to experience that. Now, virtually every sitcom on television would have to be cancelled for lack of script if sexual innuendo were to be suddenly forbidden. The non-stop use of sex as a set-up for a TV punch line has reduced what should be a grand and glorious, personal and private expression of love between a couple to the level of a Three Stooges comedy—except that the Three Stooges seemed more intellectual than today's sitcoms.

A couple entering into a relationship today has a two-fold problem on this subject of sex. First, they have been bombarded from every direction, probably since childhood, with the message that making love—"having sex"—is no more significant or special than having a good chicken-fried steak at the local diner. Second, not only have all societal restrictions—moral and cultural—been removed from extra-marital sex, it has become essentially an expectation. So much so that it can easily cause a couple to believe that if they don't immediately engage in a sexual relationship that there must be something wrong with them, or at least to believe there is nothing wrong with doing so. Problem with all that is that it has little, if anything, to do with love and pretty much everything to do with physical desire and instant gratification.

I will readily admit that the popular culture that existed when Colleen and I came of age was rather two-faced on this subject. The theme presented by Hollywood in the movies, and certainly advanced through popular music, was that of romance. In movies, the hero and heroine would chance to meet, and the girl would coyly let the guy pursue her until she had caught him. There would be close-up shots of passionate embraces and kisses, and violins would swell with the love theme from Tchaikovsky's "Romeo and Juliet." And then the lights would come up and we would all leave, thinking about what would have happened next.

But Hollywood was disingenuous about it. They would frame the shot so that a bed could be seen through a partly opened door in the room behind the couple as they made that last embrace and kiss. Or, the couple would look at each other knowingly, and walk through that door, closing it behind them. Nobody had any real doubt about what was going on—we just weren't invited in to watch.

Of course, as time passed and social mores changed, it became increasingly acceptable to enter the bedroom, to the point where it now sometimes seems to be the whole point of the movie. The subject has degenerated from being depicted as the ultimate expression of love, so personal and private that it could only be hinted at, to an up-close, graphically-filmed gymnastics event. I would not be surprised at some point to see a panel of judges seated nearby the bed, with their little scoring cards at the ready. (Would that be scoring the scoring?) It has deteriorated to the point that it can hardly be differentiated from a good sweaty game at the racquetball court.

I want to be clear, as clear as I can make myself. First of all, I am not a prude (sounds like President Nixon, somehow). I have no problem with movies having sexual content, if it is treated appropriately and with respect—and if it is germane to the story. The movie *The Unbearable Lightness of Being* was, in many respects, about unbridled lust and sexual desire. Yet, although very sexually oriented, the movie was emotionally compelling and elevated itself above the sexuality. I think it was an excellent movie. What I have a problem with is not sex, but the degree to which, and the manner in which, it has been degraded, demeaned and trivialized—and used as a substitute for a good plot and good acting.

And second of all, I'm not naive. I know that sex has been a flame that has attracted us moths since Adam and Eve. There were many cultural inhibitions and restrictions against sex outside of marriage when I was growing up. It was verboten. But it was also done. When I was a senior in high school, I had a crush on a girl in my Spanish class. She had a gorgeous figure, coal-black hair, and that mysterious, dark-eyed look of Ava Gardner. She was the only reason I took Spanish. There weren't but a few Hispanic families in my home town; I sure didn't need to be bilingual. Well, that, and the fact that I liked to read the cartoons in the back issues of *New Yorker* magazines stacked on shelves at the back of the classroom. I somehow managed to get her to agree to go to the Senior Prom with me. I never did figure out why she did that.

That was probably the most embarrassing experience of my high school career. I suppose we did dance a little, although I don't remember doing so. But it didn't take long for her to dump me and join a group that was going to a secluded spot down on the river to "have some fun." She took it for granted that would not happen with me. I didn't put up much resistance. She was right. As we Texans say, "I didn't have a dog in that fight." I knew what would be going on. She was out of my league, and I knew it.

I know there is nothing new about that. Couples "having sex" outside of marriage is nothing new. I'm well aware of that. But taking it for granted, considering it to be the norm for our culture, believing that it should automatically and immediately take place with no restrictions or inhibitions, is indeed new.

"So what's the big deal?" you might ask.

Well, here's the big deal, as far as I'm concerned. Sexual desire is probably the most powerful force on Earth, at least that exists within each of us. Ambition, greed, envy, jealousy—all the other elements of human nature are real and can be very powerful. But I believe that sexual desire transcends them all. I also believe that the overwhelming desire of sexual attraction was put in us by a God who is significantly smarter than a TV scriptwriter, and for a specific purpose. That purpose is not, as some may believe, to simply assure the continuation of the species. Nor was it given to us simply to have something more entertaining to do on Saturday night than playing with our Wii systems, or as a reward for paying for dinner on a date.

I grew up on a farm, and was around animals all the time. I know that procreation can take place quite effectively, thank you very much, with no love or personal relationship involved. The human animal is the only one for whom love and procreation are inextricably intertwined. There must be a reason for that.

That reason, I am increasingly convinced, is that it is God's way of assuring not just our continuation as a species, but also our well-being as individuals, ones that He loves and cares for. I believe a man and a woman were created for each other, and need each other. I know there are exceptions to that, just as there are to any generalization. Same-sex marriage, and feminism, raise all sorts of contradictions to that belief. And some people apparently prefer to be reclusive, seem to prefer to spend, and end, their lives alone.

But for most of us, we were not meant to live our lives alone. Our strengths and our weaknesses are complex conjugates. Colleen's strengths offset my weaknesses, and mine hers. We need each other for moral support, for comfort, for love, for assurance that we will be cared for when we need it and to help our mate when that is needed. The world can be, and often is, a lonely and fearsome place. Our life partner is our safe harbor, our port in a storm, that one person who will never hurt you and will always be there for you.

I have always believed that is true, but now that I am somewhat more advanced in age (why is it so hard for us to simply say it—I'm getting old), I recognize that we need that support and comfort even more than at any other time in our lives. Growing old is a challenge under the best of circumstances, and growing old alone is the worst of all—it is not a fun thing. Loneliness is not a good thing when you are young, and can be devastating when you are old.

Having a loving mate to grow old with you is something that can't be fully appreciated until it happens to you. And if there is no one there with you when you reach that stage of your life, it's too late to be able to make it happen. Granted, there are nursing-home marriages that make the newspapers, occasionally, but only because of the novelty nature of them. By and large, we don't get Mulligans. I wonder, at times, what some of those who so stridently denounce and resist marriage when they are young will feel about it all when they are staring into their last chapter, with no one around them that loves or much gives a hoot about them.

If all that is true, and I unswervingly believe that it is, then there must be a bond to hold us together as a couple. That bond is love, and I believe that the powerful attraction of sex was meant to be the atomic force that fuses us together in love, as one unfissionable element, for life. If that is true, and I unswervingly believe that it is, then physical love—sexual attraction—should be a celebration of that bond, a recognition of its importance in our lives, and an honoring of the God who is wise enough to have figured all that out for us and made it possible. This is the context, the framework, within which I view sex in general, and sex as it relates to marriage in particular.

Then one day I'll see a promo of some inane sitcom on TV, where the laugh-track finds the sexually oriented punch lines simply hilarious, or see previews of yet another gratuitously sexual movie, and wonder, "What the...?"

That degradation of the subject of making love from being something intensely personal and private between a couple committed to each other for life to the level of a moronic sitcom plot, or the basis for a bump-and-grind stage show by a self-appointed sex-goddess who is using sex to masquerade the fact that she can't sing particularly well, creates a whole new dynamic for couples who are just starting out in a relationship. Without question, young people today are coming into adulthood with a far different context for the subject than what Colleen and I had. Regardless of that, or perhaps because of it, they are still going to have to arrive at a mutually acceptable agreement on the subject, or expect no end to the stress caused by it.

As I stated about communication within a marriage, I will state regarding sex within—or without—marriage: There are virtually unlimited resources available to a couple who wants, or feel they need, professional guidance and help on those topics. I have no interest in, or particular qualification for, providing such help.

There are, however, two particular aspects of sex as it relates to marriage that I have some feelings about that I do want to share. Both are subjects that I believe to be of considerable importance, but which I hesitate to broach, because by this time in our society we appear to have reached the point where there is no point. The first subject is the question of sex before marriage. The second is living together before, or in place of, marriage.

But first, I have to call a time out. I recognize, and acknowledge, that in discussing these topics I stand a good chance of stepping on the toes of virtually everyone I know that is under the age of ... I'm not sure where to draw the line. So before I do that, I'd like to explain my frame of reference. Some of what I say may sound like I'm preaching—although that is not my intent—so I'll follow the example of a good sermon, and offer three points in explaining myself.

Point #1. Colleen and I recognize that the world has changed since we got married. What may have once been scandalous and forbidden has now become commonplace. We acknowledge that. Still, that does not alter how I feel about marriage and the role of sex in our lives, and the manner in which both have come to be treated in our society. I recently read *Faith of Our Fathers*, by James Bradley. His father was one of the men who helped hoist the American flag on Mt. Suribachi, during the indescribable horror of the battle for Iwo Jima in World War II.

I have had to wonder how those Marines, who survived fighting that was brutal beyond our comprehension, felt when they saw that flag being burned by students on the campuses of America's colleges twenty years later. I believe that is a good analogy for what I feel about what is happening to marriage and the role of sex in our culture. It seems to be a desecration of something I believe is important in life. It is hard for me to watch in silence from the sidelines.

Point #2. I have made reference to texts from the Bible, here and there, and I am going to do so again, here. Once again, it was written by the evangelist Paul, in a letter to the church in Rome:

> Therefore you have no excuse, whoever you are,
> when you judge others; for in passing judgment
> on another you condemn yourself.

Judging others, regardless of the topic, is a risky business. I recognize that may appear to be what I am doing. But that is not the intent of it. As I said in the previous point, what I say derives entirely from how strongly I feel about marriage, love, sex and all that stuff.

Point #3. There is a phrase in the hymn "Called as Partners," by Jane Parker Huber, that seems apropos:

> "...words of challenge, said with care."

That, I believe, is what I'm trying to accomplish. I have revised this chapter many times, trying to say what I feel, but saying it with words of care. I do hope to challenge you to think long and hard about how you feel about these topics. These are not trivial issues, and can carry a heavy penalty in emotional pain and psychological trauma if not treated with care and respect. What gets done is difficult, and in some instances impossible, to undo after the fact. So consider what I have to say on these topics to be a challenge, but they are not meant to be a judgment. That said, I'll get on with it.

Colleen and I understand the realities of our society and culture, and accept that not everything about how the way things were when we got married was necessarily better than today. All those caveats aside, we're still of the belief that having sex—making love—is the ultimate expression of love between a couple, and is best left to being a part of marriage.

We talked about it a little, while I was working on the manuscript for this chapter, and neither of us could recall that we ever had a specific conversation regarding sex prior to our getting married. It was simply not an acceptable thing to do (doing it, that is, not talking about it). Neither one of us approved of it, and we didn't allow ourselves "to go there," as the saying goes today. But that doesn't mean the problem didn't exist for us.

At that time, society simply did not condone sex outside of marriage, and would not accept the concept of a couple living together, unmarried. It's not that it wasn't done. But it certainly wasn't socially acceptable. The minister would refer to it as "living in sin," but the usual term applied to the practice was "shacking up." The problem then was the same as it is now: sexual pressures and desires brought on by the passion of falling in love are virtually irresistible—and not everybody resisted.

As mentioned in earlier chapters, Colleen moved to a college town about two hours distant from my home town to work for the summer, barely a month after we had started dating. I missed her to the point of being physically in pain, it seemed, during the week while we were separated, and she felt much the same. On weekends, I would either drive her back down to her apartment if she had come home, or would have spent the weekend there if she had not. In either case, it became increasingly difficult to separate, and for me to leave. Colleen made reference to the problem in her diary, shortly after she had first moved away.

June 11, 1956

Had the blues all day today, and felt pretty much all alone. Better this PM, but oh, how I'm missing my guy. I never thought I'd miss a guy again, but oh brother! It's getting worse.

June 12, 1956

Wanted to call Del tonight, but he called me first because he was so blue...

June 25, 1956

Was fun getting up and having my guy in town, too. He slept on a cot in the back yard. We ate breakfast and drove around until 7:00, then he had to leave and I got ready for work. Hated to see him leave.

We were both nineteen, newly in love and having to deal with the separation of her working in a town two hours away. Whether she had come home for the weekend and I had then taken her back down to her apartment, or I had gone down there for the weekend, I would stay so late that I would often spend the night. I would sleep on a cot in the basement of the house where she was staying, or out in the back yard if weather permitted. She would come to tell me good night, and sometimes that took quite a while. At one point, she wrote:

July 15, 1956

...Spent too long telling Del goodnight. We love each other too much to be as close as we were, and want to be.

The closer we became the more in love we felt, and the more difficult it became to not, as the dated '50s expression put it, "go all the way." We were isolated, had plenty of privacy, and as she said in her diary we sometimes "spent too long saying goodnight." For a nineteen-year-old healthy male, head-over-heels in love for the first time in his life with a girl he felt was a gift from God, and with Colleen feeling as intensely about me, it was a situation that was almost beyond our control.

Neither of us wanted that to happen nor, ultimately, would I have allowed myself to let it happen. My religious upbringing condemned it, but that was not the primary issue, for either Colleen or me. We both felt very strongly that we wanted to save that ultimate expression of love for our wedding night—and we did so. We were both glad then that we did, and we've never changed from that feeling.

There is one more diary entry I would like to share. I hesitated for a while before using it, because it is quite personal, but Colleen agreed to let me share it. It says more of how we feel on the subject in one entry than I've been able to say in this chapter. Note that it was written more than three years after we were married.

July 28, 1960

Gee, Del and I are so much closer now than at any time since just before we were married, and we were very close then...I was determined that I would wait, and with Del's convictions of right and wrong he would have been beside himself if he had let emotion carry him past that point with me. But my how I wish that we had stopped short of some of the closeness that we reached when we were together, then. It would have been so nice to have had some of that to discover when we were man and wife.

Human emotions, desires and temptations haven't changed much, over our history. David and Bathsheba didn't get into trouble for playing bridge together. Colleen and I were as strongly tempted by our feelings for each other as were, apparently, David and Bathsheba—or for that matter any of the bed-hopping, partner-swapping celebrities of today. Be that as it may, we both felt strongly that we wanted to wait until we were married before we allowed ourselves to make love. It wasn't any easier for us, then, than it might be for anyone today but it would appear that our priorities were different.

Easy, or not, we remain glad that we did wait. It let there be something that was supremely special between us that was only a part of us being husband and wife. It drew us closer together as a couple, as noted in that diary entry made nearly four years after we were married. For that matter, it elevated our perception of marriage itself into a more unique and special realm. I believe it contributed to the sense of bonding we have felt for our fifty-plus years together.

I would not even attempt to deny that there was back-seat activity that went on when we were in high school and college. But given that there was not much available in the way of protection, then, and that teen-age pregnancy occurred only occasionally, I suspect that there was a lot more bragging involved in the locker-room talk than a relating of fact. Even recognizing that testosterone is not a 21st-century invention, and that boys were just as desirous of being boys then as they are now, there was a cultural environment that served as a "safe-haven" for girls.

A moral element was involved that permeated our culture to a far greater degree than is true today. Good girls just did not "do it." That provided the girls who didn't want to get pressured into it some justification for not allowing it. On the other hand, on what basis could a girl possibly, in today's environment, try to convince her hot-blooded boyfriend that they should wait—even past the first date—when having sex has been made as commonplace as, oh, swearing in public, for example.

By the same token, how can that sixteen-year-old (fifteen? thirteen? Where do you draw the line, now?) boy be made to believe that he shouldn't do it, when by then he has been inundated with more bare-midriffs, cleavage, butt-tattoos, pumping pelvises, sexual innuendo and live-and-in-color bedroom scenes than could have ever been seen by an adult in earlier decades?

Colleen and I recognize the futility of our stance in today's culture. In virtually any movie that involves boy meeting girl, you can bet they will be in bed before your popcorn is gone. Read any Internet website on the subject of relationships, and ninety percent or more of the questions will involve sex—and they won't be asking whether it is permissible. And certainly none will be asking if they should wait until marriage.

So, when you have to acknowledge that by the time a girl turns sixteen she has been exposed (poor word choice, I admit) to more movies, pop-magazines, MTV routines and songs that involve sex than probably any other topic, how could she realistically be expected to believe that she should wait until she is married to engage in it? Having sex has not only been culturally diminished to the point of hardly having any more significance than holding hands, it has become a virtual expectation.

As a case in point, I was talking with an acquaintance recently and we got on the subject. He, too, is retired but had been working with teenagers in his church. He had been asked to talk with the Junior High boys about questions that they might have about dating, and what have you. He had been apprehensive about it, but agreed to do so. Keep in mind these were eighth-grade boys—barely turned fourteen. He started off by asking if they had any question they might want to ask, before he got into any of the material he intended to cover. One boy immediately shot up his hand. The very first question?

"How far should we go on the first date?"

My friend said it sort of went downhill from there.

It could be argued, I suppose, that Colleen and I are simply being "old fuddie-duddies." But I don't think so. Actually, we feel rather sorry for the kids of today. Just as they are allowed to drive in big-city traffic long before they are capable of doing so safely (and to kill themselves, and others, at an appalling rate because of it) they are permitted—virtually encouraged—to engage in the most overpowering expression of emotion that we humans can experience. And they are no more ready for that than they are to drive in big-city traffic.

Teen-age sex may not be as apt to get them killed, perhaps, but it can ruin their lives. A 2008 report by the Center for Disease Control announced that one in four girls in America between the ages of fourteen and nineteen have some form of sexually transmitted disease. One in four! Is that what our society thinks is best for our sisters and daughters? And even if they are not burdened with the problems of an STD, or teen-age pregnancy, they can be emotionally damaged by participating in something they are unprepared to handle. There are some things in life that we are not equipped to deal with until we are adults, and sex is pretty much at the top of that list. They are Little Leaguers—almost literally—playing in the emotional big leagues.

Colleen and I try to be realists. We know that our decision for ourselves is considered by many to be out of touch with modern reality. Based on some of the Q & A websites I've studied, I would imagine that if we were to make such a suggestion, such a recommendation, to a group of college-age girls that their reaction would be about the same as if we suggested that they give up their cell phones. I would like to believe that would not really be true. I want to believe that in their heart-of-hearts those same girls would somehow appreciate what Colleen and I have experienced, together, and might like to get to do the same. I would like to believe that—but I don't think I do.

In fairness to those girls, I suspect that much of the blame for premarital sex can be laid today, just as it could in previous generations, at the feet of over-sexed guys. All that I said above notwithstanding, I'm beginning to get the impression that a lot of girls agree to having sex before they are married not because they want to, but because of peer pressure and the pressure from boyfriends. And—as I said above—on what basis could our society now expect those boys to see anything wrong with doing it.

It has been encouraging that when we have talked to young couples either recently married, or about to get married, about our fiftieth anniversary they are all envious, and hope that they will get to do the same thing. So perhaps we don't differ too much in our ultimate beliefs.

What has surprised me on this topic, more than anything else, is how much more strongly I feel about it now, fifty years after we made that choice for ourselves, than I did even then. At that time, I was strongly influenced by my religious upbringing, our cultural attitudes of the time, and by my desire that I do nothing that would cause Colleen to doubt my integrity as a future husband. In other words, there was a strong moral element to my—our—decision.

Today, that hasn't really changed, but I realize my emphasis, or perception, has changed. The bond that exists between two people when they first marry can either become eroded over time, if allowed to do so, or become increasingly strong with time, like concrete setting—the longer it sets, the stronger it gets. I now realize that to have been able to share the closeness and love that we have for fifty years has created feelings that I never before experienced, or was even aware could be experienced. I believe that those feelings in some way emanate from our having kept that closest form of sharing love strictly a part of our marriage, something that has been shared only between the two of us. Call it old-fashioned. Call it passé. Call it stupid, if you're so inclined. But if you want our belief on the subject, it is quite straightforward: we believe sex was meant to be a part of marriage.

ᘓᘔ

Now. What about that other subject: living together before marriage, or as is increasingly common now, living together in lieu of marriage?

Times and social mores change, and I admit to having felt some ambivalence about this subject. I concede, first of all, that too many couples go into marriage knowing far too little about each other and what they are getting into. That's what my chapter on "Getting To Know You" was all about. The resultant problems and conflicts cause damaged feelings and, too frequently, divorce.

A traditional argument has been that any moral problems that might arise about a couple living together before marriage (although I rarely hear any moral issues raised on the subject, anymore) are more than offset by the knowledge a couple gains about each other and their ability to share a life together. If they truly aren't compatible, it is argued, it is better to find it out before the commitment of marriage and the addition of children to the problem. I understand the argument, or defense if that is what it is, that living together before marriage can be a valid way to determine if you are going to be compatible as a couple. If it staves off a later divorce, shouldn't that be considered a good thing? Sure it is, but here's the rub. It doesn't really appear to help.

By and large, cohabiting, or living together before marriage, doesn't seem to solve any problems or preclude them arising later in the marriage. An article in *The Dallas Morning News*, "Walking Down an Uneven Aisle," primarily explored the economic disparity that develops between married and unmarried couples, but also had this to say on the subject of cohabiting couples:

Cohabiting couples have the same number of hands as married couples, so they ought to make equally good parents. Many do, but on average the children of cohabiting couples do worse by nearly every measure. *One reason is that such relationships are less stable than marriages* [emphasis added]. In America, they last about two years, on average. About half end in marriage. But those who live together before marriage are more likely to divorce. . . . Two thirds of American children born to cohabiting parents who later marry will see their parents split up by the time they are 10. Those born within wedlock face only half that risk.

The National Marriage Project of Rutgers University, in its 2005 annual report on marriage, included the following statement regarding cohabiting couples and marriage:

The belief that living together before marriage is a useful way "to find out whether you really get along," and thus avoid a bad marriage and an eventual divorce, is now widespread among young people. But the available data on the effects of cohabitation fail to confirm this belief. In fact, a substantial body of evidence indicates that those who live together before marriage are more likely to break up after marriage.

The report qualified the above statement in several ways, but made this concluding statement:

What can be said for certain is that no evidence has yet been found that those who cohabit before marriage have stronger marriages than those who do not.

It would appear, then, that this "test drive" theory, as I call it, doesn't seem to be borne out in practice. Virtually every one of the young couples that Colleen and I know who have gotten married in the last ten to fifteen years lived together before getting married. Some of those marriages have turned out well. In several cases they ultimately divorced. The difference appeared to be mostly a function of the commitment of each of the couples to the marriage and to making it survive.

But of all those marriages, I would be hard-pressed to think of one couple for whom living together before the marriage appeared to have helped their marriage go more smoothly. They all seemed to experience all the same issues and difficulties as though they had not spent months living together before they got married.

So I have to wonder: What was the point of it? To rationalize living together on the basis of establishing compatibility thus seems to be a bit disingenuous, or at least misguided. First, because the results just don't seem to confirm the premise. And second, because premarital counseling and training could probably accomplish the same thing, and in all likelihood with better results because a professional counselor would be involved.

I believe that a couple will be grateful for all of their marriage if they save the "best" for after the wedding. There was a time when making love the first time after the wedding was said to "consummate" the marriage. Of the various definitions of the word, I like the one that defines "consummate" as "to fulfill." And I can think of nothing that more completely fulfills the coming together as a couple. It is a validation of the wedding vows that can be made in no other way.

It took me a while to understand what was really at the root of how I feel about couples living together before marriage. In the past, the issue was couched in terms of the moral argument. I won't make the claim that living together outside of marriage is, as it was once believed to be, "living in sin." Certainly I believed that years ago, but there is no way that I could, or would, hold myself up as being morally superior to any of the couples I've known who lived together before their marriage. That's a determination that each couple has to make for themselves, and well above my pay grade.

No, I don't believe that it is either the moral element or the "test-drive" aspect of living together before marriage that raises the questions in my mind. I believe that my biggest issue with it, at least at this stage of my life, is that I simply don't see any point in doing so, or why you would want to.

I stated elsewhere that I began to think of Colleen and me as a couple literally from the night of our first date. I told Colleen I wanted to marry her, barely two weeks later. I never once, after that first date, thought of spending my life in any context other than with her. So why would I want us to live together, and not be married?

I discuss this in more detail in my chapter on trust, but I'll summarize it here. Marriage is two things. It is, on the one hand, a legal commitment, a binding contract that assigns legal rights and responsibilities. Among other things, it serves to protect any children within the marriage, and the economic security of each spouse. The legal aspect of marriage is important and has served society well, stabilizing the family and providing a basis for the development of the children and well-being of society. That legal commitment is equally important in another way. It tells each of the couple that their mate feels strongly enough about them to be willing to make such a commitment of their life.

But marriage is much more than a legal contract. Marriage is a mindset, a point of view regarding life. It is a willing commitment, a promise that two people make to each other that they will forsake all others, entrusting the rest of their lives to each other, and loving and supporting each other regardless of circumstance. It is a choice that you make, a choice to commit yourself to another person for the rest of your life.

That's what I wanted. I wanted to spend the rest of my life living it with Colleen. So why would I feel a need to live together for a while before we formally married? Formally married was what I wanted to be. To live together and not get married would seem to suggest an underlying uncertainty, that the couple is, at some fundamental level, unsure of themselves. It suggests they are afraid that once they take that step of moving in together they will find that they are, in fact, incompatible and will want to back out.

While that seems to be, at first blush, a valid concern, it strikes me that if they are that unsure of themselves, they should first try to find out why. If the problems are serious enough, they should seek the counseling I've discussed elsewhere and try to determine the root causes. Living together probably won't address those issues or solve the problems. All it appears to accomplish is to defer those problems into the marriage, where they will still have to be confronted and dealt with. According to the *Dallas Morning News* article and the Rutgers University report, living together before marriage does not lead to stronger marriages or lower divorce rates. Facing those problems together beforehand, with a trained counselor, could possibly stave them off.

If, on the other hand, it is in fact a fear of commitment, or an unwillingness to make that commitment, that is truly at the root of one's unwillingness to marry, then I would suggest that to even want to live together is indeed wrong. You want the house, but not the mortgage. It is hard to avoid concluding that to want to live with someone to whom you are unwilling to make any form of commitment is nothing much different than wanting to rent an apartment that comes equipped with a dishwasher and a live-in sex partner.

We sometimes refer to a soldier who was killed in combat as having given that "last full measure," and in a very real sense that is how I have come to view sex. In spite of the casual, no-big-deal context that it has come to occupy in our modern culture, it is in a very real sense that "last full measure" of ourselves that we can give to another person. And to give that part of ourselves so casually, and outside the context of a life commitment, would seem to greatly diminish what we believe that part of ourselves is worth.

So I suppose that is, at least in part, what disturbs me about all this. In some troubling way it seems to diminish both what I have come to believe should be the true role of sex in our lives, and the value I place on the role of marriage in our lives. I understand the problem. Sexual attraction can be an overpowering force. But to engage in a sexual relationship with someone who has no interest in a lifetime relationship is to treat that most intimate part of ourselves as little more than a recreational activity. I have trouble believing that is a good thing.

There is a third aspect of this issue that is now becoming a developing trend, and that is for couples to opt completely out of marriage. That is, they are choosing to live together with no intention of ever getting married. In fact, from what I've read, in many cases the couple considers getting married to be more of a negative than is living together. I'm sorry, but this one really bugs me. I find little merit in that decision, or belief. It strikes me as being a dilettante's approach to life. Quite frankly, it seems little more than an unwillingness to accept the responsibilities of adulthood.

I will concede that there are probably couples who have lived together, faithfully, for a number of years without being married. I don't personally know any, but I'll accept that it could be so. But the question remains: What is the point? As the *Dallas Morning News* stated, it doesn't work out in practice. Most of the relationships don't last for more than a few years. In what way is that arrangement ostensibly better than committing your lives to each other in marriage?

If, in making such a choice for themselves, there is no expectation or even desire that the arrangement will last "for life," then the couple is treating each other basically as "disposables." In such a case, the teenage girl on the elevator in the story I told earlier would be right. It would eventually become boring. And when the relationship is no longer entertaining? Why, time to move on to another one, of course.

On the other hand, if it is expected, or at least desired, that the relationship will endure, then why the unwillingness to commit to each other in marriage? What problem is being solved, or unpleasantness avoided, by opting against marriage? It has the appearance of a "loop-hole" relationship, in which both of the couple wants to know, in the back of their minds, that there is an easy escape hatch if it is ever needed. They want the exit doors to remain unlocked at all times.

In either of these cases, the couple appears to want all the benefits of marriage with none of the encumbrances of either a legal, or publicly-stated, commitment to each other. Whether they openly admit it or not, they know they can bail anytime one or the other becomes unhappy, or bored. It seems like a cop-out.

I am reminded, on this subject, of the scene from one of the Indiana Jones movies—the one where he is searching for the Holy Grail—where Jones is confronted with having to step out into what appears to be the empty space of a deep canyon. If he does not, he cannot get to the other side of the canyon, where the Grail is believed to be. But to do so, from all that he can see, is to fall to certain death. Nevertheless, the clues from the ancient text that are leading him to the Grail tell him he must "step out in faith" if he is to find the Grail. He swallows hard and takes that first step out into the chasm of the canyon—and of course finds there is a walkway, camouflaged so as to not be easily seen, that allows him to cross safely to the other side and find the Grail.

Marriage is like that. That commitment you make, those vows you take, ask you to "step out in faith" to follow a path that neither of you can see, at that moment. But there is no other way to cross to the other side, no other way to find that "Holy Grail" that is waiting at the end of a lifetime of being bonded together. That, I believe, is the point that is too often missed. Marriage is not simply one of a list of possible living arrangements. It is that commitment to each other, that public and legal statement that you are willingly binding yourselves to each other for life, that distinguishes it from all other arrangements.

Another analogy is to compare it to the faith and trust that trapeze artists must place in each other. To turn loose of your bar is to trust your life to the partner who has to catch you. But if you don't turn loose, don't trust, nothing is accomplished. Marriage is a trust you each place in the other. You place your life in the hands of another person. Perhaps that is why it is so feared by so many today. The trust isn't there. But the prize, the Holy Grail, comes only from turning loose of your bar, making that commitment, and entrusting your life to your partner.

This situation brings to mind the movie *Defiant Ones*, starring Tony Curtis and Sidney Poitier. In the movie, two convicts escape from a chain gang. One is a white who hates blacks, the other a black who hates whites. But they are chained to each other by leg irons. If they are to make good their escape, they have to learn to cooperate. In the course of the story, they each learn things about the other, and themselves, that changes them. They learn to care for, and respect, each other. It would probably be a good movie to make a part of a marriage-training course.

Make no mistake. I'm not equating marriage to being bound together like two convicts in leg irons. But neither of those two convicts would have grown as people, in the way they did, or come to care for each other the way they did, had they not been bound together and forced to accept each other and to help each other. The commitment of marriage binds us together, and similarly forces us to learn to accept each other, and love each other, in ways that won't, or can't, happen if we know we can split at any time we choose.

I firmly believe that if a couple cannot, for whatever reason, commit to each other in marriage they should split and go their separate ways. Perhaps I'm coming down too harshly on this practice, but I have trouble finding any redeeming quality in it. Other than that, I have no opinion on the subject.

My hope, my purpose in writing this, is to offer a challenge: seriously consider such important decisions before they are irreversible. Before taking the steps of having a sexual relationship or living together before—or instead of—getting married, have a serious talk about it. Get professional counseling, if need be. If there is an unwillingness to commit to marriage, find out why. Be honest. Before taking those steps know why you are doing so, and what the emotional consequences will be.

Chapter 10

On Being a Man

Marine recruiting posters once claimed that the Marine Corps wanted "One Good Man." We tell our little boys, when they misbehave, to "grow up and act like a man." All of us guys want to be "manly" and not, as the Governor of California, Arnold Schwarzenegger, once called someone, a "girly man."

What the Marine posters didn't say—what we don't tell our little boys—is what will be required of them to be manly, what being a man means. What do they have to do to behave like a man? We do show them, perhaps without being aware of it, what we intrinsically believe it means through our day-to-day behavior and actions. But telling them is a different matter. Nevertheless, as a boy comes of age he is expected to become a man. What that means, in today's culture, appears to be a matter of dispute and disagreement.

I have tried to make it clear throughout this book that it was written to both of the couple, married or contemplating it, and not just to the guy. In this chapter, however, I am talking primarily to the guy. Colleen and I have watched as the boys we have known grew up and came of age. We have also watched, in all too many instances, as their marriages struggled and oftentimes failed. Obviously, that was not always the fault of the guy, or at least not his alone. But all too often, the guy did not seem to have a clear understanding of what being a man really entailed, especially as it related to his marriage. This is my "man-to-man" plain talk chapter.

Before I make any attempt to address this issue, and with little more than my own experience to justify the claim, I first want to offer one categorical statement about "being a man," and marriage. I believe it more completely each day my own marriage continues. It is simply this:

> Nothing else will say as much about you as a man
> as how you treat your wife and your marriage.
> Your career, your family, everything else in your
> life will be but a reflection of you as a husband.

I know, I know. Your situation is different. I just don't know what trying to get along with your wife or girl friend is like. Without doubt, some people are harder to get along with than they might be, and can subvert your every effort to do so. I recognize that, and concede the point. But I also know there are all sorts of extenuating circumstances, special situations, caveats and a lot of other things we guys use to excuse our behavior.

What I mean by the above statement is this: There aren't two sets of standards in life—one for yourself and a different set for your wife, or one for the rest of your world and a different one for your wife and marriage. And quite frankly, we've seen all too many guys behave in their marriage as though they don't understand or believe that.

It is, to put it plainly, hypocritical to excuse in yourself behavior you won't tolerate from your wife. It is delusional to think of yourself as an honest man while cheating on your wife. If you can permit yourself to cheat on her, and lie to her, you can do it to anybody. It is disingenuous to attempt to present yourself in public as a considerate, caring person and to then go home and be short-tempered, intolerant and inconsiderate to the person you presumably love more than any other. I'll say it again: How you treat your wife is the most accurate measure there can be of yourself as a man.

Perhaps that all sounds a mite on the harsh side. I suppose, at least in some ways, I intend it to be. Colleen and I have seen too many instances, and have been adversely affected too many times, by guys who didn't seem to believe it, or want to accept it. Nothing I say in this book will be of any value to any guy who does not accept the truth of what I said above. And everything I say is, in some sense, predicated on that belief.

So, having said that, what is a "real man?" How should he conduct himself? What characteristics would best define him? Is there some litmus test that can be applied? (I suppose the actual chemistry lab litmus test strip would be appropriate—it turns pink or blue.) When you tell your son to "grow up and act like a man," what are you expecting of him? If you had to write down the top five characteristics of being a man, what would be on your list?

Our traditional cultural stereotype of a "real man" was probably best exemplified by the "Marlboro Man" used in the hugely successful cigarette advertising campaign of years ago. He was virile, ruggedly handsome, steely-eyed, firm-jawed and sat tall in the saddle. His Stetson was pulled just low enough on his forehead that you knew this was a man you did not cross.

His Marlboro cigarette drooped casually from a corner of his mouth just the way John Wayne used to do it. You knew he could handle himself, wouldn't take any guff off anybody—and he probably spoke in one-word sentences. His face was on billboards over Times Square, and we all knew that's what a real man was supposed to look like. Of course, he probably died prematurely from lung cancer, but no one talked about that.

Is that it, then? Is that what we mean by being a man? But what if nature didn't bless you with rugged handsomeness, and no matter how hard you squint and clench your teeth, you just can't seem to look steely-eyed and firm-jawed? You've never been in a saddle in your life and wouldn't know if you were sitting tall in it if you were in one. And furthermore, you're a compulsive talker. Does that mean you have all strikes against you in the "manly" department?

Ask any two people what it means to be a man and you'll probably get three or more definitions, none of which agree. Ask a cattle rancher in Montana, or a steel worker in Pittsburgh, and you'll probably get different answers than if you ask a professor at Harvard University, or the president of the National Organization of Women.

Not only that, our societal perception of being a man, of manhood and man's role in society and marriage have changed substantially just over my own lifetime. When I got married there was no question but that the Marlboro Man, the John Wayne, husband as head-of-the-household stereotype was what most people would have envisioned if asked what a man should be. But then along came the feminist movement, and from it the derisive comment attributed to Gloria Steinem (who disclaimed credit for the phrase) that became a source of contention: "A woman needs a man like a fish needs a bicycle."

This movement not only held the traditional view of manhood in total contempt, but questioned whether there were any redeeming qualities to the male of the species at all, aside from his unavoidable necessity for procreation. I grew up in a culture that would get you chastised if you didn't hold a door open for a lady, and matured into a society where women would supposedly be insulted if you did so.

So—was I being a gentleman for attempting to hold the door open for a woman, or a male chauvinist pig for suggesting that she was too weak and incapable of doing it herself? I stopped worrying about it, years ago. I was taught to be courteous, so I always hold the door open regardless of who may be entering or leaving, male or female. How the person reacts to it is up to them. Interestingly enough, I've never been taken to task for it, and always thanked.

My own views about manhood have evolved somewhat over my years. During my teenage years, the concept of manhood was clearly defined. We were shown examples in every movie. I mentioned them before: John Wayne, Gary Cooper, Gregory Peck, Charlton Heston—all were "real men." We all knew what a man looked like and how he conducted himself.

A real man was the head of the house, the bread-winner. He brought home the bacon—and expected his wife to fry it. He talked softly—if at all—but carried a big stick, or a Colt forty-five. He won wars, knew how to get the car running again and fix the bathroom faucet. There is no doubt but that these cultural stereotypes and patterns influenced me as I grew up. And in many respects, they still do.

At the same time, there was no small measure of male chauvinism intrinsic in the mindset of the men around me as I grew up. It was clear in the clichés of the time. Men who succumbed to their wives "nagging" were "henpecked." You have to have raised chickens, or at least been around them a lot, to fully understand how disparaging that term was to a man. It was openly wondered of such a man, "Who wears the pants in that family?"

My dad was a hard-working man. He did his utmost to provide for his family during the Depression, and we never suffered from want of food or from any real hardship. He was always good to Mom, at least in the conventional sense. I never once heard him raise his voice to her. While she was bedridden, the last three years of her life, he cared for her day and night with little help and without complaint.

But in normal times, when Dad came in the house, his day's work done, he expected supper to be on the table and it almost always was. When it was over, Dad went into the living room to read the paper, or doze a few minutes, while Mom did the dishes and cleaned up. Dad would require us kids to help with the dishes some of the time, but I don't remember ever seeing him do any dishes, or any other housework.

Dad, I'm sure, never gave it a thought. He was no different than any of the other men we knew. In fairness, once Mom became bedridden, and we kids were long gone, Dad did all the household duties. But while both he and Mom were healthy the division of duties was clear.

A man's role was to earn the living—once he walked in the house his job was done. On the other hand, if help was required doing chores, or in the field, the wife was expected to come out and lend a hand. I don't know how Mom felt about it. She may have felt that it was a little unfair, but if so she never mentioned it to us kids. It was generally accepted as the norm for marriage, at the time, and certainly so on a farm.

Fortunately for my own marriage, I somehow seemed to recognize that double standard from when we were first married. Not long after we were married, we had a brief dust-up over something quickly forgotten, but Colleen had written about it in her diary that night. The fuss we had didn't get much mention. I knew she was worn out from studying, and had insisted she take a nap after we had cleared the air.

What bowled her over was the surprise awaiting her when she got up. She wrote, "When I got up, Del had done up all *my* dishes." The italics are mine. It surprised me, when I read that comment decades later, that she had taken it for granted that *our* dirty dishes were *her* responsibility. She fully expected that they would be waiting for her when she got up from her nap. She said something very nice about me in her diary after that, but I'll not include it here.

Everything that I believe is true about marriage derives in some fashion from my conviction that it must be a partnership. Colleen and I had our occasional flare-ups, but never in our marriage did either one of us feel that we were not equals in the relationship. We have changed how we handled the work load, depending on circumstances, but I don't believe either one of us has ever felt we were carrying more than our fair share. All that not withstanding, there was no small amount of my cultural patterning in my own mindset, especially in our early years of marriage.

Without question, society's concept of what is expected of, or required of, a man has changed from what was true for earlier generations. The traditional role of being the "bread winners" of the family is no longer the sole responsibility of the husband. Women are now, by and large, equal partners in that. As a result, both child care and domestic chores must also now be shared. Fixing meals, giving the kids their baths, cleaning the house, all chores that were the sole province of Mom when I was growing up, are now considered tasks to be shared equally by both spouses.

I used to do all the mechanic work on our cars, from oil changes to rebuilding the engines, but no more. Our automobiles are so sophisticated that very few people can do any real "shade tree" mechanic work on them, so fixing the car has also been removed from the list of Dad's duties. Little mechanical skill is required to take the car to the local lube shop for an oil change, or leave it at the dealer for servicing.

I don't know if marriage experts would agree with me on this, but I am of the opinion that one factor in the tremulous state of matrimony today is the fact that in many respects the guy no longer knows what, in fact, is expected of him or what his role should be. Certainly, most of the traditional roles of men in a marriage would seem to no longer apply. But guys are still guys; we still want to be thought of as being a real man.

So—back to the original question. How would I define how a "real man" would conduct himself in a marriage? While working on this chapter, I asked Colleen one evening, while we were having a bite of pizza, what one word, one characteristic, she believed would best describe a "real man," in the context of a marriage.

I had already chosen the one word I would use, and suspected I knew the one she would choose. She hesitated, at first, to answer. She knew I had been thinking about it for some time, and I had hit her cold on it. But after giving it some thought, she responded with what I was sure would be her answer: "I would say, 'fair.' I think a real man would be fair to his wife."

I smiled at her and said, "That is precisely the word I had chosen, and thought that you would choose. It's no wonder we got married."

It isn't necessary, I believe, to go to a dictionary to define "fair." We all implicitly understand what it means. But I think, for my purposes here, I will use the word in the context of paraphrasing the Golden Rule—treating your wife the way you expect her to treat you.

I am going to make quite a bit of this point. You may think I'm overstating the point, or making too much of it. But Colleen and I have seen too much unfairness in too many marriages to be able to believe that too much can be made of the point. So, even if you think I'm not being fair, bear with me on it.

A real man is fair. I think most of us would probably agree on that. But there is so much wrapped up in that one word that it is hard to know where to start. I also said earlier that I grew up believing that real men were tough and courageous. And that's true. In life, a man does need to be tough. I don't mean tough in the sense of being harsh, or able to whip any challenger in a fist fight. I mean resilient, able to take blow after blow and keep on with the struggle. Life throws a lot at us, and you have to be able to stand up to it, deal with it. You have to be tough. A lot of what we have to deal with in life is unpleasant and rather daunting.

But if he is to be fair, a real man has to be toughest on himself. You can't expect things of your wife that you are unwilling to expect of yourself. You can't allow yourself excuses that you are unwilling to accept from your wife, or grant yourself privileges that you are unwilling to grant your wife.

To be fair, a man has to be courageous. We normally associate courage with physical risk, the courage shown by soldiers in combat or the courage shown by the fireman who enters the burning building to save a trapped child. But there are other forms of courage, and a married man must show them daily. It requires courage to get up every morning and go to a job that has long since lost its appeal, because your family needs you to do it. It takes courage to not allow your daughter to go on the date, when you know she's too young but she is angrily insisting that she is not.

Being fair also requires another kind of courage. It takes courage to tell your buddies you aren't going to play golf on Saturday, because your wife has had a hard week and needs a break. It takes courage to admit that you are at fault in a disagreement, courage to apologize, courage to "fight fair."

But knowing all those things, and doing them, are two different things. It isn't always as easy as it sounds. As important as "being fair" has always been to me, and to my marriage, I got a very pointed reminder while writing this that I was not always able to do so. Colleen had found a box of memorabilia (one of many we have accumulated) from our early days, and we had been looking through some of it when I found a collection of letters we had exchanged around the time of our fourth anniversary. I had largely forgotten about them, but they opened a window into our past. I quickly became engrossed in reading them, enjoying reliving a time that marked the end of our college years and the beginning of our real life together. That is, I enjoyed them until I read one that really jolted me.

After I graduated, I took a job in New Jersey with the Bell Telephone Laboratory. At the time, the Lab was responsible for the development of the Nike Zeus Missile Defense System. Zeus was America's first attempt to defend itself against Russian ICBM warheads. The task was often described, not inaccurately, as attempting to shoot a bullet with another bullet. Our group was in charge of the design of the guidance package in the missile.

We had a basic, unsolved problem at the time. Before launch, the Zeus missile was in an underground cell, out of sight of the radar system that steered it while in flight. A means had to be found for coupling those radar signals into the cell before launch, until the missile was out of the cell and in view of the radar. That challenge became my first real engineering career assignment.

All the missile testing was conducted at White Sands Missile Range, a vast no-man's land of desert located in southern New Mexico. The nearest city was El Paso, Texas, nearly sixty miles from the base. It fell my lot to go to White Sands for several weeks to conduct tests on the various systems we had conceived as possible solutions to our radar problem. And that's where my marriage became affected by all this.

Colleen and I were coming up on our fourth anniversary. Our college years had been daunting. We were looking forward to our new life in New Jersey as an opportunity to finally get to be a real married couple, with enough income to finally afford us a little breathing room. We had also, in our first four years, never spent a night apart—and we very much liked it that way. We were unequivocally not ready emotionally for weeks of separation. But separated we would have to be, so we decided it would be best for Colleen to spend the time staying with family in Kansas.

So, barely six months out of college, I found myself staying—alone—at a hotel in a West Texas border town that I knew only through Marty Robbins' hit song, "El Paso." I was to be working on a task that, until then, no one else had resolved. I knew nothing about radar—had never seen a real one until I got to the base the first time—and little about the missile system I was to be testing. I was also going to be required to negotiate test time with the radar group and the launch cell union crew, both of which had bigger fish to fry than my little tests and weren't disposed to interrupting their work to support mine.

I think it would be easy to guess my frame of mind at the time. I told Colleen in a letter to her, weeks later as the testing neared completion, that I felt I had been thrown into a den of lions and left to fight my way out. Without question, I felt intimidated by it all, but assumed my boss wouldn't have sent me down there unless he believed I could handle it. My biggest problem was not the technical challenges. It was that I was not one bit pleased about us being separated for weeks, now that we were just beginning to be able to enjoy being out from under the pressures of college. As I headed for El Paso, I felt I was headed for some place well past the intersection of no and where, and was not a particularly happy camper.

Keep in mind this was in January 1961. Long distance telephone calls were expensive, and infrequently made. I was not permitted to make any but the most essential and cursory phone calls on my hotel bill. Colleen was reluctant to impose them on our parent's phone bills, and we certainly couldn't afford very many of them. They were expensive enough that Colleen referred to them on one occasion in her diary: *"Talked to you nine minutes last night—was marvelous to hear you, but not sure we can afford it."*

It was such a different environment. Now, we would just call each other on our cell phones and talk as long as we desired. But it was 1961, not the twenty-first century, and we were resigned to staying in touch just as all previous generations had done—by letter. So it was not enough that I would be, as another old country and western song put it, "sleeping single in a double bed"—we would be largely out of touch.

Colleen was an inveterate letter writer. She wrote lengthy, newsy and personal letters to virtually everyone she knew—parents, friends, relatives, anyone she believed would want to know of our comings and goings. I, on the other hand, was cut from the same bolt of cloth as my parents. Letters from Mom and Dad were of the "How are you? We are fine." variety. Such was my background, and that's the type of letter I tended to write.

So the unfairness started right there. Colleen and I shared everything we did, but we were always together to do it. I loved to talk to her, and it seemed we never stopped. But if I had been required to get acquainted with her by letter it would probably have taken six months for her to learn my middle name. I would receive long letters from her, filled with all her doings and telling me how much she loved me and missed me, and she would get back a short letter to the effect that the testing was really not going well, I was pooped from a 14-hour day of it, and would try to write a bit before turning in, signed "Love, Del." (You can see why she is now quite incredulous that I have written a book.) I did try to assure her, a couple of times, that there were all sorts of things I wanted to share, and could hardly wait until we could be together again so I could talk to her—but she didn't get any of it in those letters. She never complained about the inequity of it. She just expressed her joy at receiving each of them.

As I was reading through those letters of hers to me, I found one that simply stunned me. It was written just after I had first arrived at the base, and she had not yet received one from me. We don't either of us remember, now, what the problem might have been but she had gone to the expense of a long-distance call to me, anxious to learn if I had made it to El Paso all right.

In her letter, written just after we had ended the call, she was devastated, and worried half sick. According to her letter, during the call I was short, impatient and would scarcely talk to her, volunteering little and answering her questions with noncommittal one-word responses. She said I sounded as if it had been an imposition for her to have called me, or even that there might have been someone else in my room that I didn't want to hear our conversation. She even confessed at the closing of her letter to feeling jealous, wondering if I had a girl in the room with me. Her letter to me, after that call, was so full of anguish that in reading it, forty five years later, I was mortified. I was, in fact, so embarrassed by my behavior those forty five years earlier that I took the letter upstairs where she was doing something or other, asked her to read it, then told her how sorry I was that I had ever done such a thing to her.

We talked about it a while. Bless her heart, she had long since forgotten all about it and was surprised by the tone of her letter to me. I tried to imagine what had been behind it all. At the time I had arrived in El Paso I was only twenty four, fresh out of college, and I knew that I was in over my head. I had been sent down there alone, so had no one from work who was more experienced to turn to for assistance or guidance. I had never before been separated from Colleen, was lonely and probably, if I would have admitted it, a little scared of what lay before me. But nothing in all that could have justified what I did to her.

I know what the real problem was, now that I look back on it through the lens of forty five years of maturing. It was just all one big pity-party for myself. I was feeling sorry for myself. I wanted her to feel sorry for me. She was feeling as lonely as I was, and knew how I was feeling. But given her nature, I'm sure she was trying to cheer me up by sounding cheerful, positive and upbeat during the phone call. But I wanted her to be as blue and despondent as I felt, so I could believe that she missed me as much as I missed her. She probably didn't let herself sound that way, just for me—to keep me from worrying about her. So, being a guy and doing what guys tend to do, I behaved like an ass.

We did get it all sorted out. My boss let me fly up to Kansas the following weekend to see her. It was the weekend of our fourth anniversary, and I most certainly did not want to spend it alone in El Paso, Texas. I don't recall whether I told my boss that it was my anniversary weekend, or not—I probably did, to press my case for the trip—but in any event it was very perceptive of him to let me go. I think he knew what they had tossed me into, and knew I would need a morale boost. In any case, the visit let us resolve whatever had transpired between us, and put some salve on the wounds.

We had a joyful anniversary weekend reunion, and the tone of our letters was much improved after that. In fact, I sent one to her a few days later while she was visiting our old friends at Kansas State that, she told me in her letter back to me, left her with a dreamy smile on her face and too choked up to talk for a while. She said our friends just left her alone until she could talk again. So I guess I in some way redeemed myself.

As luck would have it, that letter was not among the ones we found so I didn't get to read what was apparently one of my better ones. In any case, the event became just one of those things that a married couple has to work through, and faded into the yellowed pages of those letters to stay there until I rediscovered it, and got to be embarrassed by it, more than four decades later.

What was so terribly embarrassing to me about that episode was how completely unfair I had been to her, when I would have adamantly insisted that I was a very fair person. As I said, fairness means simply being the way toward another person that you would want them to be toward you. And Colleen had been caring, considerate and thoughtful to me. She had written me lengthy letters, had phoned me and tried to cheer me up. And for that, she got treated in the most selfish and thoughtless manner possible, and needlessly hurt. By any definition or standard, I hadn't been fair.

My point should be obvious: it doesn't really matter how badly you feel your life is treating you at the moment, or how much you might believe you deserve the world's sympathy. In all likelihood, it was not your wife who put you in the situation. And, just as likely, she is the one person trying hardest to help you through it. Be fair. Think of her. Be as considerate of her as she is of you. Maybe, then, you won't feel you need to apologize to her decades later for being such a jerk. It's either that, or don't let her keep your old letters—destroy the evidence.

Included in the photo section is a still of Gary Cooper, in his role as Marshall Will Kane in the movie *High Noon*. That still, and the movie, are classics. The movie has virtually all the elements, good and bad, of human nature. There is the evil of the men coming to kill the Marshall, the spinelessness of the citizens of the town, who refuse to take the personal risk of helping him in his time of peril. There is the courage, honor and integrity of the Marshall, the love of his wife, the understanding of the female friend who knows him better than his new wife does. If you want to understand America, at least at that time and in many respects even now, just watch that movie if you haven't already. Cooper's portrayal of the Marshall has become an icon of what a "real man" was supposed to be.

In the movie, Marshall Kane learns virtually within minutes of his marriage to his stunning new bride (played by Grace Kelly, who was beautiful in ways that modern actresses don't even perceive) that three men he had sent to prison have been released and are on their way to town to kill him for revenge. Their train is to arrive at "high noon."

The marshall is, first of all, pragmatic—an attribute I would include on my "real men" list. He recognizes immediately that it is pointless to run. They will pursue him until they catch him, and kill him, if he permits it to happen. He knows he has to face them.

He is sensible, and not guilty of false bravado—another item on my list. He returns to town, and attempts to get his deputy and various of the town folks to help him confront the killers. But they are cowards, and refuse to put themselves in harm's way to help him—that's why they pay him the big bucks, is a paraphrase of their response. He knows he is on his own.

He is patient, gentle, kind, and understanding—all important items on my list. He does not rail at his wife when she pleads with him to not go back to town, or accuse her of being too dense to understand that the killers would just track them down. He patiently and gently explains the futility of his running, and why he has no choice but to return. When his deputy and the townspeople won't support him, he does not blow his stack at them or accuse them of being cowards. His reaction is one of understanding and resignation, rather than lost temper and anger.

He is courageous—a biggie on my list. He knows, when the train has arrived and is chuffing its way out of town, that he is soon to face death. At the far end of the main street through town are three men coming toward him, with the express purpose of killing him. But he doesn't run. He is willing to face what must be faced.

He is smart. He knows there is no hope in facing the three of them directly—he will certainly be killed. So he is stealthy, and attempts to get them one at a time from a protected position.

Of course, as the plot plays out, it takes some unexpected twists. His new wife has to quickly learn, first of all, trust. She learns that the town "shady lady" is truly a friend to her husband, and that as a friend she can love him without being a threat to the marriage. His wife also learns that she has to have her own brand of courage. And finally, she has to make a choice between her own pacifism and her husband's life.

That movie was released in 1952, when I was sixteen years old. It probably did more to shape my perception of what adulthood entailed, of what it meant to be a man, than any other single influence on my life, at least at that time. I matured hoping that if I ever was placed in a similar situation that I could be the man that Gary Cooper was in *High Noon*.

The courage of the Marshall was never in doubt. The question I have had to contend with, though, is this: Have I wanted, all these years, to pattern my life after a man who could not be fair to his wife? To face the killers, rather than run for his life, would in all probability make his new wife a widow before she had changed out of her wedding dress. Was it fair to her, to do that?

I've said that marriage should be a partnership. There was no "partnership" here. He didn't ask her for permission to face the killers, or give her a vote. He didn't accede to her pleas to run, to leave it to the town folks. Was that being fair? Realistically, he had only two options. He could do as his wife pleaded with him to do and run for his life. Or he could return to town and face them. He took what he knew in his heart was his only real choice.

He knew from his experience with evil people that to run was the worst choice and the one that would truly be unfair to his wife. He knew they would never know a moment of peace in their lives, would not have a life, so long as the killers were alive to hunt him down. And he knew they would do so. He knew, therefore, that he had no realistic alternative but to face them.

I have never been confronted with such a choice. But I have been put in situations, or have put myself in situations, where I had to make a choice to stand for what I believed, or not. There is a poem by James Russell Lowell, *The Present Crisis*, that has a statement that appeals to me. The poem dealt with the Civil War and the issue of slavery. The lines are:

> "Once to every man and nation comes the moment
> to decide / In the strife of Truth with Falsehood,
> for the Good or Evil side...."

Those lines, and other parts of the poem, were made into the hymn, "Once to Every Man and Nation," that is included in the hymnal of our church, which is where I first became aware of them. They have weighed heavily on me, at times, and I've tried to keep them in the back of my mind while trying to decide how I would deal with some of my own difficult choices.

In making the choices that I did, I sometimes put Colleen and myself in situations that were unpleasant and difficult. Was I being unfair? I don't know if I consciously thought of Gary Cooper and *High Noon* when I made my choices, but I believed that to fail to take the stands that I did would in very real ways diminish me as a man, and as a husband. That, I believe, would have been even less fair to her.

So, a real man, a good husband, is fair to his wife. Recognizing and accepting that fact is oftentimes easier than acting on it, but it is essential to a marriage that one never lose sight of it. In every interaction between a couple, that principle must be the guiding light and the basis for all actions and decisions. If you aren't sure of yourself, uncertain about some decision you are about to make or some action you are about to take, then talk it through. You have to remain true to your principles, but in the final analysis you must also be fair.

There is one last aspect of this subject of manhood that I feel compelled to mention, but find hard to write about. That is the subject of maturity, or the lack of it. The unwillingness of too many young men of current generations to grow up, to leave adolescence behind and become an adult—"become a man"—is a real phenomenon confirmed not only by my personal experience but by recent surveys of the young men themselves.

I've lost track of the specific survey, but one I read not so long ago had the majority of guys who were surveyed admitting that they didn't believe they should have to "grow up" until sometime in their mid-to-late thirties.

A recent article by *Time* magazine—"Grow up? Not so Fast."—deals with the topic. A researcher who had been studying the phenomenon was quoted as saying, "Legally, they're adults, but they're on the threshold, the doorway to adulthood, and they're not going through it."

The problems that result from the failure of young men to enter "the doorway to adulthood" are manifested in many real, discernible and often painful ways.

The difficulty with trying to discuss this is that it immediately suggests a generational one-upmanship contest. It strikes of being a cartoon, of two old geezers wheezing to each other on a park bench about the "sorry state of youth of today," and trading "I had to start plowing with a team of mules when I was only three years old..." exaggerations.

Older generations have always thought that the youth of their day were going to Hell in a hand basket, to use an old expression. Witness the following:

> The children now love luxury; they have bad manners, contempt for authority; they show disrespect for elders and love chatter in place of exercise. Children are now tyrants, not the

servants of their households. They no longer
rise when elders enter the room. They contradict
their parents, chatter before company, gobble up
dainties at the table, cross their legs, and tyrannize
their teachers.

From what I've been able to learn, that statement is attributed
to Socrates, by Plato—well over two thousand years ago. I don't
really want to be guilty of doing the same thing, at least not just
for that reason.

The fact remains, however, that young men of today are finding
few compelling reasons to stop acting like adolescents and to start
"acting their age." Virtually every young guy I know, or have had
occasion to have to deal with, has shown evidence of the attitude.
It would require some effort to think of one I have personally
known who seemed very eager to take on the responsibilities and
behavior of adulthood until well into their thirties.

There are probably several factors that contribute to this
issue. One is that there are fewer societal, or cultural, factors that
force young men to take on the role of adult at an earlier age.
Earlier generations inevitably had to face the military, as our
country was constantly involved in some form of war or combat.
Another factor was economic. Sons were required to contribute
to the economy of the family by assisting with farm work, or
getting a job. This happened, especially on the farm, by the time
the boy was big enough to carry a bucket.

I won't argue the safety aspects of it, but I was driving a
tractor doing field work before I was ten years old. My cousin was
killed doing the same thing before he had turned fourteen, but Dad
didn't take me off the tractor when it happened. By the time a boy
turned eighteen and officially came of age, he was expected to get
a job, leave home and be on his own. I don't know of a single male
my age who ever moved back in with his parents after he had left
home. It was pretty much unthinkable.

Another factor, I think, was our cultural perceptions. As
I discussed above, our cultural male icons, our heroes, when I

was in high school were the John Wayne/Gary Cooper crowd. By the time my own sons were coming of age, they were watching John Belushi as 'Bluto' Blutarsky in *Animal House*, or Chevy Chase in *Caddyshack*. I admit those movies were funny, and have enjoyed watching them. (Well, I enjoyed *Caddyshack*. I can do without *Animal House*.) But what a different image of manhood is presented by Gary Cooper in *High Noon*, and John Belushi in *Animal House*.

This could all be laughed at, taken to be nothing more than the natural competition between generations as was supposedly expressed by Socrates, if it didn't result in so much real pain and trouble. A young woman I am close to had to suffer through two divorces because the two guys simply would not grow up and assume the mantle of manhood required of being a responsible husband. One of them, when I asked him why he was bailing out of the marriage, whined, "I'm just not happy. I guess I'm not ready to grow up." This sounds distressingly similar to the story I told of the girl who derided being married for forty years to the same person as being "boring." I guess marriage really is supposed to be entertaining, now.

I talk elsewhere about the problems that result from "a failure to communicate" in a marriage. I believe that what we have here, in a very real and growing sense, is a "failure to grow up." Like it or not, by the time a young man has reached the age of twenty, it's time he starts getting serious about life and "grow up"—become a man.

Perhaps the most eloquent, beautifully phrased description of love is from the New Testament of the Bible, in the 13th chapter of the first letter of Paul to the people of the church in Corinth. If you've not read it, I suggest you do so. In that letter, Paul also speaks to this issue of maturity. His message is just as apropos today as it was two millennia ago:

> "When I was a child I spoke as a child. I under-
> stood as a child, I thought as a child; but when I
> became a man I put away childish things."

Paul had it right. When you become a man—and I don't care what the surveys say, by age twenty you've become a man—it is time to put away childish things.

There is an aspect of this belief—that it acceptable to put off adulthood until one reaches his mid-to-late thirties—that goes beyond the problems and stresses caused to others by the lack of maturity. That is the waste of what is typically the best, and most productive, time of a person's life. Most of the real accomplishments of a person's life usually occur in his first two decades of adulthood—his twenties and thirties.

Einstein was twenty-six years old in 1905 when he published his special and general theories of relativity, and two other papers, that revolutionized physics. Mozart died at age thirty-five, having composed over 600 pieces of some of the world's finest music by that time. Blaise Pascal, the seventeen century scientist and philosopher, accomplished enough that we still remember him four hundred years later—and he died at the age of thirty nine.

It's not that we don't, or can't, accomplish anything of note at a later age. There are countless examples of accomplishments by people in their sixties, and even as late as their nineties. Nevertheless, we are far and away at our productive peaks from age twenty to age forty. We are healthiest, have the most energy, our brains are at their peak capacity, and we are the most enthusiastic.

From age twenty, when Colleen and I got married, to age thirty five—the time when guys are now saying they should begin to take on the role of adulthood—Colleen and I had three college degrees between us, three kids, had bought a house, sold it and built a new one in the country. I was well into my engineering career, had my pilot license and we were serving on church boards and local school boards.

I'm not saying any of that to brag, although I am proud of us for having done all that. The point of it is that we could not have accomplished all those things if we had waited to start until we were thirty-five. We simply would not have had the time, energy, stamina or motivation to do in our fifties all that we had done by our thirties.

Our career years are typically age twenty to age sixty-five—forty five years. To start at age thirty five is to pass on one third of your available career. Why would you want to do that? We talk of how much longer people live, now, and how they expect to do all those things later in life. That's true. People are living longer. But just because more people are living into their eighties and nineties doesn't assure that they will be physically capable of having an active career at that age. It's not as easy for me, in my seventies, to toss a football with my grandson as it was at thirty-five to toss one with my young sons.

This whole late-maturing situation brings to mind the lyrics from another song:

"I'll never grow up, never grow up, never grow up,
Not me,
Not I,
Not me!
So there!
Never gonna be a man,
I won't!"

That's right. It's from the movie *Peter Pan*. Those lyrics seem humorous when sung by a make-believe fantasy-character in a Disney movie. But when it becomes the mantra of a healthy, intelligent male in his prime years of coming-of-age, it's a little hard to swallow.

We are granted an opportunity in this life to make of it what we will. But we don't know how long our stay on this planet will get to be. We all assume that we will live to a ripe old age, and the odds are with us that we will, in fact, get to do that. But to fritter away ten or fifteen of the best years of your life, not wanting to take on the role and responsibilities of adulthood because it isn't any fun, seems at best a waste.

So, time to wrap this up. What does it mean to be a real man, then? This is a hard issue to summarize. Trying to define a real man is not much different than trying to define a beautiful woman. We all believe we know one when we see one, but trying to describe her in words fails the reality of it—not to mention the old saw of beauty being in the eye of the beholder. Even though it may seem hard to define, honesty, integrity, trustworthiness, courage, fairness, kindness, patience, gentleness, responsibility, resilience, all are attributes I think we could agree on.

I mentioned above the passage by Paul in 1st Corinthians, chapter 13, on love—and included a portion of it that talked about maturity. I am going to paraphrase a different portion of it here, substituting "A man" for where Paul used "love." I believe it says more in one paragraph about what a "real man" is supposed to be, than I've have been struggling for pages to say. Paraphrasing Paul:

> A man is patient, a man is kind. A man does not envy, a man does not boast, is not proud. A man is not rude, is not self-seeking, is not easily angered. A man keeps no record of wrongs. A man does not delight in evil but rejoices with the truth. A man always protects, always trusts, always hopes, always perseveres

I don't know what more could be said. Paul does mention one characteristic I didn't specifically mention above, although I consider it to be important, and that is perseverance. A real man perseveres. He doesn't cut and run at the first sign of trouble—or the second, or the third. He is always there, ready for duty. He is less concerned about sitting tall in the saddle, and more concerned about getting back in it when he's been bucked off. He makes every effort to apply those principles discussed above to his life, every day of his life, learns from his mistakes, and doesn't let the occasional failure to do so keep him from trying to do the right thing the next time.

Chapter 11

Trust

"I do solemnly swear that I will support and defend the Constitution of the United States against all enemies, foreign and domestic. . . ."

Each year, thousands of American men and women join the armed forces of the United States. When they do so, they have to take the Oath, which begins with the statement above. Also each year, well over four million American men and women take another kind of oath, in which they pledge to get married "'Til death do us part," or "As long as you both shall live."

There is a certain degree of irony between the two scenarios described above. When an inductee takes the Oath, no specific mention is included of pledging to literally give their life in the line of duty, if so required. And yet, that possibility is implicitly understood. Although it may not be directly stated, the inductee accepts the fact that he is joining an organization whose very reason for existence may expose him to being killed. My cousin paid that price in World War II, and many hundreds of thousands of other citizens before and since have paid the same price.

In contrast to that, during a marriage ceremony each of the couple typically vows to "give their life" to the marriage. I would suspect, however, that at the time they make that pledge, neither of the couple is giving much thought to the fact that they are literally pledging their lives to each other and to the marriage.

Both of those events—marriage, and joining the military—contain both a legal commitment and a personal commitment. It's rather obvious why joining the military, either voluntarily or through the draft, includes a legal commitment. An army can't be built based on a group of individuals who believe they are free to bolt when the shooting starts. The question is, why is there also "the Oath?" Why ask that person to pledge to do something that he is already being legally required to do, and can be imprisoned for failing to do?

I think the short answer is that it is a matter of commitment, and trust. A military leader has to know he can trust his troops under fire. When the shooting does start, the outcome of the battle depends on the level of commitment of those doing the fighting. The threat of being imprisoned for failing to do your duty doesn't mean much in the face of the threat of death.

A more interesting, and paradoxical, question is: Why does a marriage ceremony include either a legal or verbal commitment? That is, why does marriage require either a legally binding contract or a personal pledge to each other? It would seem, on superficial inspection, that if a couple wanted to spend their lives together, they could simply do so. Why all the fuss and bother of legalities and public professions of commitment?

Apparently, a growing number of people are asking themselves that question, and answering it in the negative. That is, they have concluded there is no value in either a legal or "word of honor" commitment. They just start living together, with no intention of having a wedding or getting legally married. As I stated in an earlier chapter, such a decision is not a good life choice. In most instances, the relationship does not survive for more than a few years.

Why is that? What is there about that legal contract, and the personal pledge, that makes marriage the most enduring, and the most rewarding, choice we can make regarding how we spend our lives together?

In an attempt to answer my own question, I'll state first that I believe the legal aspect of marriage is essential and accomplishes two things, both quite valuable. The legally-binding contract of marriage is a statement by each of the couple that they feel strongly enough about the other to be willing to be legally bound to them.

It is a statement of trust. But in the event that trust was misplaced, the legal contract is also protection, assuring that neither can be unfairly treated by the other. It also makes provisions for any children within the marriage. Those two aspects, the symbolic statement of trust and the protection of a legal contract, serve as an important foundation for the relationship.

The second element of a marriage ceremony, the personal pledge that each makes to the other, is also important and essential. Those vows are not just symbolic. Again, it is a matter of commitment and trust. When you face your marriage partner and vow that you will love, honor, cherish, and support him or her regardless of life circumstances, as long as you live, you are literally pledging your life to that person. You are pledging your word of honor. And your spouse places his or her trust in you, believing that you are a person whose word can be trusted. That personal pledge, those vows you make, are no trivial matter.

It is no small thing to neglect, or shun, those two facets of marriage. To expect to share a life together, but be unwilling to accept either the legal contract or to make the public statement of commitment, raises awkward questions about the way you view each other. I believe that is why such living arrangements don't endure. Sooner or later, that unwillingness to commit to each other will manifest itself in some aspect of the relationship, and when that happens there is no basis then for it to survive. The relationship doesn't—can't—endure, because neither person was willing to commit themselves in any fashion to the relationship. There is nothing binding them together, and at some basic level neither can trust the other.

The consistent theme, the common denominator, of all that I've said above about marriage is trust. Everything in marriage is predicated in some fundamental fashion on trust. I've discussed throughout the book those elements that I believe are the essential building blocks of a successful marriage. But if those elements are the building blocks from which a good marriage is built, then trust is the foundation on which that marriage rests. Marriage is a commitment. That commitment is predicated on trust. Once that trust is betrayed, it is excruciatingly difficult to recover, and often pretty well lost forever.

We form a number of relationships in our lives. We form friendships, we join organizations, we affiliate with political parties, and so forth. Each of those, in its own way, requires a degree of commitment and has its own form of interaction and responsibilities. Yet, none of those compares in the manner in which they involve every element of our personality as does a marriage. And none is as predicated on trust as is marriage.

We trust in many ways, sometimes without giving any conscious thought to the matter. We trust that the pilot of our airliner is skilled and will deliver us safely to our destination. We trust that the surgeon knows what to cut, and what not to cut, when we go under the knife. That is more a personal trust. We may not actually know our pilot, or surgeon, but we can identify them as people—we can talk to them, be reassured by them if we so choose.

We may never meet them face to face, but we also trust the engineers that designed the bridge we trust our lives to each time we cross its span (or at least we did before the Mississippi River bridge in Minneapolis collapsed). We trust the designers of the elevators that whisk us hundreds of feet above the ground. We don't know those engineers, but we trust them, nevertheless.

In all these cases, however, trust has a means of being verified. We can, if we are inclined to be paranoid on the topic, ask to see the pilot's license. The surgeon's office wall is plastered with certificates assuring us that he is qualified to do our surgery. The elevator we ride on has a certificate of inspection, certifying that it is safe to ride on. So we trust, but it is not a "blind" trust.

Marriage is not like that. We agree to devote our life to an individual based solely, and entirely, on that person's "word of honor"—or at least on our perception of that person based on the time and extent to which we have come to know them. Still, there is no certificate, complete with embossed Seal of the Great State of Wherever, stating that our beloved has met all the requirements and conditions pertaining to the state of matrimony and is duly certified to be trustworthy.

Instead, we stand before a minister, a priest, a rabbi or justice of the peace, whomsoever we choose to perform our ceremony, and look each other in the eye.

"Do you...?" asks the official.

"I do," he says.

"Do you...?" the official asks again.

"I do," she says.

"Okay, then. You're married," states the preacher, priest or whoever.

And on that basis we commit our lives, all the remainder of our years, to that person to whom we just made that promise. Nothing else we do in life can be compared to that.

On our currency we say that "In God We Trust." But in our marriage we state that "In you I trust." And the success of that marriage, that relationship, is based entirely on that tiny filament, that silver thread of trust. If that filament ever breaks, if that thread comes unraveled, it can never be truly restored. There may be attempts to superglue it back together, but like Humpty Dumpty, you can't really put it back together again—at least not in its original, undamaged form.

More than anything else a marriage can succeed only so long as there is trust. You may believe that you like and respect your mate. As a husband, you may try to communicate well and try to behave like a man. You may both do all the things I've talked about elsewhere in this book. But if at some fundamental level one of you finds that the other cannot be trusted, none of those things will much matter. And it is directly proportional. The greater the trust, the greater the marriage. The poorer the trust, the poorer the marriage. There is no equivocating that point.

Permit me to digress from my topic of "trust," for a bit. I promise I'll come back to it. I mentioned earlier that marriage is one of the seven sacraments of the Catholic Church. It is not a sacrament in our Presbyterian church, but it is considered to be a religious ceremony and commitment. The wedding service generally includes the minister telling the couple that they are being joined in holy matrimony with the stated, or at least implied, admonition that we are to consider that our union is blessed by, and sanctioned by, God. Consequently, a couple would be promising not just to themselves, but to God as well, to be faithful to each other. That, as my mother-in-law used to say, makes the cheese more binding. (I never really understood what that old saying meant, but it sounded serious.)

We were married in my home church, and our wedding service was clearly a religious ceremony. We believed in and accepted that religious aspect of our marriage, but I never gave too much thought to it. My view was rather simplistic, in a sense. I knew I wanted to spend my life with this girl who had so captured me. I had a pretty strong moral component to my feelings, and would not have considered anything but marriage as the way to get to spend my life with her. And she would not have permitted anything else. If our union was blessed by God, so much the better. But all I really wanted was for us to be married. I wasn't afraid of the commitment of marriage. I wanted us committed to each other for life, with no prospect of separation. Marriage was how you did that, so that's what I wanted.

I grew up in that church. Colleen framed my church "cradle roll" certificate (so old it looks distressingly like parchment) and hung it on a wall in our hallway. My social life centered on the church as a teen-ager. So I would never have considered anything but to be married in that church. I took it for granted that our wedding service would be religious in nature. Nevertheless, if I had given any real thought to the religious aspect of marriage, at the time, I probably would have assumed that the early churches had instituted marriage as a religious ceremony primarily to help assure its success, its longevity. I could have imagined some medieval priest telling some young serf, "Now, don't you go cheatin' on this young maiden, boy, or God will smite you for sure."

To my knowledge, there aren't but about three places in the New Testament where Jesus is quoted talking about marriage, and most of the quotes seem to have more to say about divorce and adultery than with marriage, per se. There is one passage that does speak to my point:

"Have ye not read, that he which made them at
the beginning made them male and female, and
said, for this cause shall a man leave father and
mother, and shall cleave to his wife: and they
twain shall be one flesh?"

This would seem to suggest that God did, indeed, sanction
marriage (I'm using the term as derived from the Latin, *sanctus*,
to sanctify). None of the Protestant denominations that I was
aware of had established marriage as a sacrament, so I had rather
assumed that the God-sanctioned aspect of marriage was, in fact,
primarily a man-made construct created by the hierarchy of the
organized church.

But in truth, I don't think I gave it much thought at all. I think
I just accepted it, and took it all for granted. Now that Colleen and
I have spent the better (and I mean that in both "the larger part
of" and "superior to all else" senses of the word) part of our lives
together, I'm finding that I have developed a view of marriage
that is far more complex than was that simplistic view I had as a
twenty-year-old infatuated with my new love.

I find I am beginning to believe that the church has it right. I
believe that marriage truly is, or should be, a spiritual experience—
because I can't find any other explanation for how I've come to
feel about it. I've tried to think of some other things we do in
life that are comparable in some way to a good marriage and find
that I can't think of any. It has been elevated in many ways in my
thinking, to the point where it seems almost mysterious. There has
been a strong spiritual, or religious, element to marriage throughout
much of history and in many cultures. I think I understand now
why that is true.

That religious nature of marriage was experienced by Jonathan
Edwards, the Revolutionary War era minister, in his marriage. In
the quote of his dying words that I include in the last chapter,
Edwards referred to his marriage as an "uncommon union," and
said that it "...has been of such a nature as I trust is spiritual and
therefore will continue forever." Apparently, Edwards had come

to the same belief that his marriage was spiritual in nature, blessed and sanctioned by God.

Marriage is an "uncommon union," a strange institution, when you think about it. Why would two people agree to separate themselves from the rest of society, and agree to completely dedicate themselves only to each other, for all of their lives? Yet, that is what we do. We agree to love only this one person, to make love with only this one person, to share all that we have and are, only with this one person. It is strange. Yet, that is the way we function best as individuals and as a society. Thousands of years of civilization have continually corroborated it.

Now, back to my original topic of "trust."

If marriage were like many other activities or ventures we are involved in during our lives, if it were no different than, say, joining the Rotary Club or your fitness center for a few years, then it wouldn't matter so much whether it lasts, or not. That was the point of my digression, above. Marriage is, or certainly should be, an experience and commitment that is above and beyond the norm of our daily activities, elevated to the level of being perceived to have a divine nature. It is a lifetime commitment, and one not to be taken lightly.

But that agreement to commit ourselves and our lives to another person, for the remainder of our lives, works only so long as both of the two people believe that their life is safe in that commitment. In other words, only so long as they can trust that person to not betray them.

I described in an earlier chapter how I had hurt Colleen by being so unpleasant—so unfair—to her when she had called me while I was at White Sands Missile Range on my first job assignment. In a letter she wrote after that call she even wondered if I might have had a girl in the room with me. After we had talked about that letter, after I had made my forty-five-year-belated apology, I had to ask her,

"Did you really believe that I might have had a girl in the room with me—that I would have done such a thing to you?"

She shook her head.

"No, of course not. I've always known I could trust you, and never thought otherwise. I don't know why I wrote that. I probably just wanted to shake you up, and let you know how much you had shaken me."

I didn't really think she would have thought that of me, but it was reassuring to hear it. That is one thing that I feel best about, where our marriage is concerned. We always trusted each other implicitly, and neither one of us ever gave the other one a reason to doubt that trust. While I worked for a large electronics firm in Texas, I was required to travel quite a bit, so would be away from home for a night or two, or on occasion for a week, or two. During that time I stayed in motels and could have found a way to "have company," if I had been so inclined. Of course, she was at home alone (after the kids were older—it's kind of hard to do too much hanky-panky when you have three little kids around you) and could have done the same. But neither of us ever remotely considered doing so.

I must, at this point, interrupt myself to tell a story on us. Around the time I turned forty, we learned that several men we knew had been caught having affairs. There was a cheap motel, not far from where I worked, that was notorious for being the place where those trysts took place. Colleen and I would occasionally joke about it as we drove past. On my fortieth birthday, she picked me up at work. As we came to the motel, she pulled into the entrance.

"What's going on?" I asked, looking more than a little surprised. She just smiled at me, and pulled to a stop in front of the motel office.

"Well, it seems a lot of guys are having flings around their fortieth birthdays," she explained with a grin, "and they all come here to do it. I was afraid you might be feeling a little jealous, so figured I'd better get it out of your system. So, you're having your fortieth birthday fling tonight. You're just having it with me. The kids are spending the night with the neighbors. We're already booked. Why don't you go in and get the room key?"

It's pretty hard to want to be unfaithful to someone like that. I believe that one of the reasons our fiftieth anniversary seemed so

meaningful to me was, at least in part, because of the recognition
that we neither one ever gave a reason, or was given a reason, to
doubt that we could trust each other.

And that brings up the corollary topic, the antithesis of trust,
of infidelity—that stake-in-the-heart of any marriage. I suppose
I should spend some time dealing with the subject, but in truth I
have very little to say about it. Infidelity is the ultimate betrayal
of the trust I talk about above. I have, at times, tried to imagine
how I would have reacted, how it would have made me feel, to
learn that Colleen had been unfaithful. My mind simply won't
wrap itself around it. In all probability, our marriage would have
been destroyed, right along with the trust that we had shared.
Couples we have known have had to deal with it, and some of
them found a way to forgive and try to salvage what they could
from their marriages.

Of course, that is as it should be. Those couples are to be
commended for doing so. But I don't think I could have handled
it. Maybe that's why my feelings are so bluntly simple regarding
infidelity. I believe that it is wrong from any, and every, perspective.
I believe that it is morally wrong. If you accept the spiritual nature
of marriage that I discussed above, then infidelity is a sin against
God, as well as your spouse. And if you don't buy those aspects of
it, then it is wrong simply from the broken-trust nature of it. You
vowed that you would be faithful. So infidelity not only breaks
the trust between the two of you, you also break your own solemn
vow—your word cannot be trusted.

I cannot imagine how any married person, male or female,
can believe that infidelity is acceptable or can be justified under
any circumstance. If your marriage is that unacceptable to you,
then why not do what has to be done to find out why, and solve
those problems? Why not fix your marriage? If that can't be done,
then get divorced. Infidelity is the ultimate failure on the part of a
spouse, the ultimate denial of the trust your spouse placed in you,
and the ultimate rejection of the person you vowed to love. In
what context could that not be considered wrong?

Chapter 12

Be Prepared

Being married is a bit like being a Boy Scout—you need to adopt their motto, and "be prepared" for all that you are going to experience. I don't mean that in the sense of a warning, as though you are approaching dangerous territory, or some emergency. But any endeavor in life goes better if you know what to expect and are prepared for it. And few of us know that, going into marriage. That was certainly true, in many respects, for Colleen and me. As most couples have to do, we worked it all through. I am now of the opinion, however, that there are better ways to do so than we sometimes did.

Old Dog, New Tricks

It occurred to me at times, while I was growing up, that if using clichés in daily conversation had been declared illegal my parents and all my relatives would have been rendered mute. There seemed to be a cliché for every situation. Two of them, that I heard rather frequently, were (1) "You can't teach an old dog new tricks," and (2) "You're never too old to learn." Their contradictory nature didn't appear to cause a conflict for anyone, but it did make me wonder: Well, which is it? When I get old, will I not be able to learn anything, or will I always be learning new things?

I'm now officially old, and the verdict is in. Cliché #2 wins; you're never too old to learn. That has proved to be true in most aspects of my life, and certainly has been true in my marriage. One of the areas where I feel I have gained considerable new insight, mostly while working on this book, has to do with what marriage specialists might call "conflict resolution."

Colleen and I know couples who we simply could not imagine ever having a real argument, or fight. For example, I mentioned our friends, Dosie and Pop-Pop, who were the Godparents of our three kids. They both seemed so genteel and proper, so refined, that I couldn't imagine them ever arguing or fighting with each other. I'm probably wrong about that, but so it seemed. We weren't like that. We did, in fact, have some real disputes, at times. The fact that we did so always bothered me, sometimes rather deeply. It seemed so inconsistent with how I knew we felt about each other. Finally, now, this old dog has learned some new things about the subject, that have been very enlightening. I'll try to explain.

To do so, I need first to refer again to a book I mentioned in the Introduction called *Why Marriages Succeed or Fail,* by Dr. John Gottman. I found his book to be especially informative on this topic. Dr. Gottman describes himself as a research psychologist, trained in mathematics. I guess the engineer in me responded to that description.

In the book, Dr. Gottman relates that in the 1970s he realized there were simply no scientifically-based data on why marriages succeeded or failed, so he set out to correct that lack. He set up an instrumented marriage "laboratory" at his university and recorded all sorts of data on married couples who agreed to be his "guinea pigs." After twenty years of such research he claims to be able to predict with 94 percent accuracy whether a particular marriage will succeed or fail.

Two very interesting—and to me, highly surprising—conclusions offered by Dr. Gottman in his book are:

1. A certain degree of negativity is crucial to a marriage. Without it, a marriage will surely deteriorate over time.
2. You must have at least five times as many positive as negative moments together if your marriage is to be stable.

I was impressed with Dr. Gottman's findings, at least in part, because my nature and training as an engineer relates to conclusions based on scientifically determined data. He based his conclusions not on personal opinions or conventional wisdom, or even psychological theory, but on carefully recorded and analyzed reactions of married couples placed under typical marital stresses.

The most striking conclusion, and the one that resonated most with me, was his statement that some negativity—whether it be arguments or even getting angry at each other—not only did not have to represent a threat to a successful marriage, but in certain respects was essential to it. Obviously, my next question was, "Okay, but how much negativity is acceptable, before it begins to destroy the relationship?"

Again, I was impressed that he could offer a quantitative answer: there has to be at least five times as many positive moments in the marriage as negative. Fall below that threshold, and the marriage is probably in trouble.

Dr. Gottman's observations struck at the heart of the concern I expressed above. There were two or three subjects about which Colleen and I had significantly different attitudes and beliefs. We would attempt to discuss them, but at times the discussions would escalate into more serious disagreements—we got pretty upset with each other. Those spats, as she called them, seemed to have two elements to them.

First, there was the obvious aspect of simply being ticked off over the disagreement. That was expected, and seemed to dissipate rather quickly, most of the time. Once we had hashed the issue out, we usually got over it fairly quickly and in short order I usually couldn't remember what we had fussed about. But some of the times, there would be a second element to those episodes, that seemed to disturb me far out of proportion to their significance.

For one thing, I was embarrassed for having let them affect me the way they did, and to have allowed them to get me as upset as would sometimes happen. I was also apprehensive that it would somehow cause Colleen to lose her respect for me, or to even stop caring for me. My behavior was the antithesis of what I had seen of my folks, and I was afraid that I was damaging my relationship with her.

What she could never get me to comprehend was that she had grown up in a household where arguing was common between the parents, and she was quite accustomed to it. She assumed that it would blow over and we would just get on with things. No big deal. She told me any number of times that she thought of them as the waves on an ocean. The surface might be stormy, but beneath it all was miles of quiet calm.

My problem was that my growing-up environment was the complete antithesis to that. I never once heard any of the grown-ups in my extended family have an argument, or even raise their voice to each other. A Hayes just did not do that. Certainly not in public, or even in private, for that matter. I never once had an argument of any consequence with my parents. Thus, when they took place between Colleen and me, I had no context for them. Her reassurances were helpful but still didn't make me feel any better about the fact that they had happened.

Now I learn that having those arguments was probably necessary in order for us to air and resolve our differences, for we did come to a better understanding and agreement about them, over time. Probably, without those disputes, the issues would have festered beneath the surface until they exploded into real problems. Or, they would have simply eroded the feelings we had for each other. I wish it hadn't taken most of my married life before I learned that, but it helps to know it now. So, the issue that then tweaked my engineering curiosity was how we had measured up to the five-to-one positive-to-negative ratio required for a good marriage.

I wondered for a time how one would measure that. If you had a two-hour set-to, then went the rest of the day getting along fine, that would be twenty-two hours "positive" to two hours "negative"—an eleven to one ratio. But that didn't seem realistic within the context of what Dr. Gottman was meaning. I realized that we could have had some sort of problem one day a week and still had a ratio of six good-days to one not-so-good day. That alone would have met his criteria. Even when we were under the most stress while in college and seemed to get on each other's nerves too frequently, and during the stressful years of raising our kids, I don't believe we ever let it happen that often. I suspect that I am in large measure simply guilty of "analysis paralysis" on the subject.

In spite of all that, the subject wouldn't completely go away for me, and I wondered why. I finally concluded that it was because I know, in retrospect, that I could have, and should have, done a better job of dealing with the disagreements. I believe much of my inability to do that at the time was a result of the fact that we had so little training—we weren't "prepared." We were never shown, at least very well, how to do a better job of resolving our differences.

Dr. Gottman's assertions about the necessity of some negativity in a marriage notwithstanding, it pains me, now, to have to accept the fact that I let our disagreements happen the way they did. We were talking about it recently, and I admitted my disappointed in myself for not learning to find a way to rise above them, and handle them better than I did. I accepted the fact, as she suggested it, that I was not solely at fault, or responsible. She contributed her fair share. Still, I told her, I was the biblical head of our household. It was my responsibility to find a way to let us resolve our disputes in a positive manner, and I sometimes couldn't seem to do that.

All of which leads me into my next subject.

Marriage Training

It can easily appear, at least on the surface, that having a successful marriage is a complicated and difficult task. In certain respects, that's true. For two people to live together for most of their lives without stress or conflict is not an easy thing to do. Witness to that fact are all the "how-to" books, radio and TV talk shows all on the topic of how to make a marriage work. All that notwithstanding, I will be so bold as to claim that being able to have a successful marriage can be deceptively simple. Let me take a stab at explaining myself.

I'm being a bit on the facetious side when I say this, but I now believe there are just two basic rules for having a successful marriage. Those rules are:

1. Play nice.
2. Follow the Golden Rule—it will get you most of the way down the road to a golden anniversary.

I'm joking—it's really more complicated than that. Or is it? I am convinced that if you marry a person that you genuinely like, and love them, are nice, respectful, fair, considerate, tolerant, patient, kind, civil and exhibit all the other aspects of human behavior that you desire and expect from that person for yourself, then a happy, lifetime marriage is virtually a guaranteed certainty. I don't know how any person who loved you at the beginning of your relationship would ever lose that feeling for you if treated in such a manner. Indeed, I suspect your spouse would love you even more at the end of that fifty-year time together than when you said, "I do."

Put another way, I don't believe that Colleen and I ever had a fuss caused by my being too respectful, too fair, too kind, too considerate, too patient or too tolerant. We only had problems when one or the other of us was perceived as not being fair, not being considerate, appearing not to care, and so forth.

So it <u>was</u> simple. It just wasn't easy. On the contrary, both of us found it all too easy on occasion to get wrapped up in our own egos and expect from the other what we were unwilling, at that moment, to give in return. When we could get past those feelings of pride and wounded ego, and begin treating each other again according to my Rules #1 and #2, things would get back to the way we both wanted them to be.

It may appear that I am talking out of both sides of my mouth here, but I'll try to differentiate. As Dr. Gottman states, some negativity, having arguments and disputes, is essential to a healthy marriage. On that basis, it would seem I should just blow it all off. Shrug my shoulders, and say no big deal; it was good for us.

But I suspect that attitude can be used to justify copping out. I believe we each have a responsibility to do our best at getting along with everyone in our lives, and certainly so with our spouse. To justify a needless argument on the basis of "it's good for us" is taking the easy way out, and ultimately bad for the relationship. So, I still felt compelled to better understand this issue.

The question for me became: If marriage is as simple as I stated above, then why did we have the problems we did? Why were two intelligent people who loved each other unconditionally unable to do a better job of handling disputes than we sometimes did? We are both by nature considerate, respectful, caring people who would never intentionally hurt the other. So what was really behind those times when we would get crosswise with each other?

To answer my own question, I have had to conclude that we, and probably most married couples, are inadequately prepared for what will be one of our more challenging life experiences. That is especially true when compared to the training we receive for many of the other areas of our lives in which we may be involved.

Consider, for example, what I had to go through to become a private pilot. The simple act of flying an airplane is not terribly difficult. It is possible, after only a few hours of instruction, to be able to take off, fly around the airport, and make a safe landing. But to become a licensed pilot, capable of flying sophisticated modern aircraft in today's complex air traffic control environment with its myriad regulations and demanding procedures, in all kinds of weather, and do so safely is quite another thing.

It required two years and scores of hours of training to be able to get my basic private pilot license. I had to pass a three-hour, closed-book exam and an hour-long test flight with a government inspector-pilot. More years and hours of training, and another difficult exam and test flight, were required to be able to safely and legally fly in instrument conditions; more hours to fly a multi-engine aircraft. Every two years I have to demonstrate to an instructor that I still meet basic qualifications to continue to legally fly.

Now that I have done all that, now that I have endured the endless hours of training, have passed the exams, have re-qualified time and again with flight instructors, now that I am approaching two thousand hours of flight experience, flying seems rather simple. I know what to do and how to do it. Much of it now seems second nature, and I can do it with little conscious thought.

So it seems to be with marriage. Now that I have fifty years experience, the requirements for a pleasurable, rewarding marriage also have become second nature. The most significant difference between these two examples, obviously, is the issue of training. To start with, it is not legally possible to fly today without being certified by the Federal Aviation Administration. To get that certification requires that the applicant undergo all the training mentioned above.

Conversely, a couple can appear before a Justice of the Peace and in a matter of minutes be legally married—no training required. No tests. No instruction. Just pay the license fee, take the vows, and you're married. You can now spend the rest of your life trying to learn how to do so properly. If you're lucky you'll learn the lessons and develop a stable and happy marriage. Otherwise. . . .

I confess that in promoting the concept of marriage training that I am urging others to do something that I would have been highly reluctant to do myself. The reason for that is the same reason people—especially guys—are reluctant to do so today, and that is the stigma associated with it. In the first place, it's usually referred to as either counseling, or therapy. And who wants that? Any form of counseling or therapy carries with it the connotation of either a personal failure or deficiency of some sort, or even mental illness.

When we got married, what would now be called a mental health hospital was then called various derogatory names, from "looney bin," or "nut house," to the official name of insane asylum. You didn't have a mental illness, then—you were insane. You were crazy, nuts, looney. It was necessary that such a person be isolated from society, hopefully never to be seen again. That's why they were put in "asylums," and not hospitals.

With that public perception, few would ever willingly admit to any form of problem that might smack of a mental condition. To admit that you might need, or want, counseling was to admit that you were "crazy." I know of no one at that time who voluntarily sought any form of counseling for marriage, or for anything else, for that matter. It was simply unheard of, at least in our neck of the woods.

But look at the consequences of that negative societal attitude regarding preparation for marriage. The divorce rate, and the number of couples shunning marriage in favor of cohabiting, are stark testimony to the risks of entering into marriage with no training or preparation. There is virtually nothing else we do in life—not in our careers, or even in our recreational activities—where we expect to be able to be successful at a challenging venture with no advance preparation or training.

Yet, we base the success of our marriage on the presumption that we know all we need to know the day we say "I do." But how could we possibly know anything of consequence about marriage, based only on what we superficially observe of the few married couples we experience as we grow up. The simple answer is that we can't, and we don't, know much at all.

I have the impression that we treat preparation for marriage not unlike what I experienced playing football in high school. Our coach was a passive, uninspired and uninspiring sort who seemed to have lost all his competitive spirit years earlier, assuming that he at one time had some. He drew X's and O's on the board for us to learn the plays, describing them in his monotonic drone that mostly put us to sleep.

Practice consisted largely of blocking against a blocking dummy, held by another player, trotting through dry runs of plays, and wind sprints. On occasion, but too infrequently, we would scrimmage. The traditional protocol was that you got to suit up and warm the bench as a sophomore, substitute occasionally as a junior, and start every game as a senior. This seemed to hold true

more or less independent of your level of performance relative
to others on the team, unless there was no one available to fill a
particular position. Then you got to start as a junior.

Thus it was not until my senior year that I got to experience
very much of the reality of the game. I had to learn to deal with
the fact that, unlike the blocking dummy, the opposing lineman
would fight back and would knock you on your keister if you
didn't learn to fend him off. I had to learn how to hold off the
offensive lineman, and still be able to get a shoulder into the gut
of the running back coming through the line behind him and drive
him into the ground. By the end of the season I had learned to
handle myself pretty well, and could hold my own against most of
the guys I came up against.

Our last game had been against our hated rival school from
the adjoining county. We had led most of the game, but lost just
before the end of the game because of an interception run back
for a touchdown (why our quarterback threw a pass to the sideline
when we were ahead with time running out, I'll never know). We
stood there for a few moments in disbelief, then the guys began to
walk off the field, heads down, back to the locker room. I couldn't
bring myself to leave. I stood there, alone in the middle of the
field, absorbing the emotions flooding over me, oblivious to the
fans filing silently out of the stadium.

It was one of those crisp October nights, the kind of night for
which high school football had been invented. Chilly, moist air
made your nostrils tingle as you breathed deeply after the exertion
of a tough play. Dew had already begun to form on the grass on
the field. I loved the feel of air that was nudging toward frostiness
but didn't seem cold, the musty smell and the feel of damp earth
and grass. It began to settle over me, to penetrate my bitterness at
losing the game, that I would never again stand on a damp, grassy
field on a crisp October night like that, and play football.

I had come to love the game, and the exhilaration of making a
jarring tackle, or springing our halfback with a textbook block. For
high-school-aged boys whose testosterone levels were soaring, it
was an outlet that had no peer. Football had helped me gain a lot

of self confidence. I felt much more sure of myself. A lump began to form in my throat, and I had to blink back tears. I knew I wasn't within rifle-shot of being able to play at the college level. For me, high school football would be it. I realized then that this was the end, the last of it.

It seemed so wrong. I felt that I had spent all that time learning how the game was to be played, learning how to handle myself and to do my best. It seemed that all those games I had played had been just prologue. I wanted to be able to say, "Send me in, coach, I'm ready"—and my last game had ended. My career was over and I felt I was only then truly prepared to play.

The feeling was not terribly different from what I have come to experience regarding marriage. I've spent fifty years learning what it takes to be a good husband, a friend and companion to my wife, and father to our children. And now that I feel qualified, trained and ready, I see that my "marriage game" is well into the fourth quarter, with time running out.

In marriage, as in football, it would seem to make a lot more sense to be better trained before the game starts.

It's in My Genes

You perhaps have noted, by now, a common theme in all that I've said on this subject up to this point: All the issues I've discussed are behaviorally based. That is, our problems were a result of our behavior, and our behavior is our responsibility to control. If we are not conducting ourselves the way we should, then it is up to us to change our behavior. It is all a matter of will. As I suggested above, it follows from that premise that better training, better preparation, for marriage could reduce or eliminate most of our problems.

There is no doubt that I have believed essentially all my life that how we behave is a matter of will and is our personal responsibility to control—in our marriages or any other aspect of our lives. But as has happened on a variety of subjects, as I've aged and gained more insight and perspective on life I've been forced to accept that things generally aren't so cut and dried as I believed when I was young. And that has happened on this subject. I am now not so certain that all that we do is "simply" a matter of will and choice.

These issues are in some sense a subset of the long-standing "nature vs. nurture" argument that I mentioned earlier in the book. That is, do we behave the way we do because of how nature constructed us, through our very DNA, or is it because of the way we were raised, or trained to be? With respect to marriage, are our problems a result of the fact that we are simply "hard to get along with," or are we hard to get along with because we are hard-wired by our DNA to be difficult, argumentative, combative, whatever?

For most of my years, I have been strongly in the "nurture" camp. I was raised in an environment where a person was considered to be responsible for their own behavior. Bratty kids were "spoiled" and needed a good spanking. Wives that were difficult to get along with were "shrewish" and "contentious." Husbands were "no-accounts," or "just plain mean." If you were upset, down in the dumps or otherwise had some emotional problem, you were just supposed to suck it up and "git over it."

There is a lot of me still in that camp. I believe modern society is all too quick to blame our behavior on some syndrome or disorder so we don't have to accept responsibility for ourselves. I have tended to have little patience with people who thus appeared to be trying to shift the blame away from themselves to some vague sense of "the devil made me do it." I now find myself leaning toward a more balanced perspective, and am of the opinion that we are complicated combinations of both elements. That is, we are indeed products of our upbringing, our "training," with respect to how we conduct ourselves. But I believe we are also products of how we were created, slaves in some sense to our very DNA. The problem, of course, is discerning which is which.

I have wondered for years why the problems Colleen and I had occasionally loomed so large to me, and affected me so disproportionately. Most of the time we could work out our differences without too much fuss and bother. We might get rather annoyed with each other, but usually, within a few hours we literally couldn't remember what the fuss had been about and things were back to normal.

But on some occasions, something would happen to cause us to get crossways with each other and I would get unduly upset about it—far out of proportion to what it was worth. Once the fuss came to an impasse, I would feel myself sinking into what felt like some form of depression. Although these periods would usually be triggered by the arguments that we would get into, at times they seemed to come from problems outside the marriage. They would typically last for 24-48 hours. I could feel myself sliding into them, but felt powerless to stop it from happening.

Colleen would attempt to console me, at least most of the time. Occasionally, she would become exasperated and get frustrated with me. I would then get defensive, sometimes combative, add guilt to the depression and go even deeper into what we called my "blue funks." They would on rare occasions last nearly a week, but usually after a day or two something would snap in my mind, I would say basically "to hell with it" to myself, and it would be over.

I'd apologize for causing the problems, she would insist that no apology was necessary, tell me once again about stormy waves on a quiet ocean, and we would go happily on with our lives. Until the next time it happened. During those episodes, I was the antithesis of the person I normally was. I had no self-confidence, couldn't let myself believe that Colleen loved me, and was largely a dour, depressed and unpleasant person. We never found a way to deal with them very well. I guess we just tolerated them.

Writing about all this, I must confess, was not particularly a fun thing. I do so for two reasons. The first was because I suspect that Colleen and I were not—are not—alone in having to contend with such issues in our marriage. And second, I do so because I now believe that there was more going on for us than we had any way of understanding.

In recent years I have become acquainted with people who have been diagnosed with bipolar disorder, and are on medication for it. They are completely different people when on medication compared to when they are not. Obviously, their behavior is more than just a matter of "will." Having seen that, I have begun to wonder if I had some mild form of something of that sort.

I am not a trained specialist, and don't play one on TV, so am only guessing. Maybe I'm making this all up, looking for an excuse to justify my behavior. But I do know that those periods—whatever their cause—seemed to be totally out of my control to keep them from happening. I do find it interesting that it has been years since I experienced one of those episodes of any significance. I have to wonder if my body chemistry changed, over my later years.

This all leaves me feeling decidedly ambiguous. That is, I have a problem deciding what is a real medical, treatable problem and what is simply a failure to assume responsibility for your behavior, and to seek a crutch to lean on.

It has become somewhat the popular thing to do in our society to ascribe some clinical sounding name to what used to simply be accepted as part of human nature. We don't have behavior problems, we have "disorders," or "syndromes." Small boys have, since the dawn of creation, preferred running and jumping to sitting still, and being boisterous to being quiet. Yet, when they now get unruly when expected to sit quietly at their desk for extended periods, we say they have "attention deficit disorder" and drug them into compliance.

If it's just a normal problem, it is up to us to solve it ourselves. But if it rises to the level of a disorder or syndrome, then it's not our fault. I have been inclined to believe there has been a certain amount of aggrandizing and blame-shifting going on in all that. It is much easier to blame some official-sounding disorder than to admit that we are simply being immature or self-pitying.

That personal beef aside, I recognize now that everything about us, from our most fundamental bodily functions to our most elevated thoughts and emotions, are in truth nothing but complex chemical reactions. Our brains are, in simplest terms, little more than complicated chemical plants. Every thought, feeling and action that we experience is in some manner the result of chemical processes occurring in our brains.

It doesn't seem unreasonable, then, to believe that altering those reactions, changing the chemistry, could affect our behavior. We see the concept manifested daily in the way drinking and doing various drugs affect our personalities and behavior. It would thus seem that looking to the medical profession for clues to our more intractable behavior problems is not outside the realm of reason.

I have wondered, in recent years, what the effect on our marriage would have been if this condition was something that could have been detected, diagnosed and treated early in my life. If due to some mild chemical imbalance, it would probably have been treatable. It is discouraging to think that at least some of those difficulties could possibly have been avoided.

The entries in Colleen's diaries that talk about my getting into those spells, and the problems that resulted from them, are hard to read—but we had no basis for understanding what was really going on. A person was just expected to "get a hold of yourself," and straighten up. Colleen and I were both solidly in that philosophical camp. But, at least while it was happening, I felt incapable of doing it.

If this is true, if we are to better understand how we get along in our marriage, then we must look at both our preparation for marriage—our training—and at our own nature. For most of the years of our marriage I felt a strong sense of responsibility—read "guilt"—for the problems that Colleen and I had. Because of that, I've come to the conclusion that we need far more "training" for marriage. But I've also begun to acknowledge, especially as I've come to know people with bipolar disorder and similar problems, that at least some of our behavior is clinically, or medically, based. And those issues need a physiological solution. You can be trained to better deal with being bipolar, but it can't be "willed" away. It has to be treated.

One could argue, obviously, that not everyone has some "mental illness" so why would marriage counseling be necessary in those—probably majority—cases? My rebuttal would be to point to the popularity of radio talk shows featuring marriage counselors such as Dennis Prager and Dr. Laura, and to the hundreds of books on marriage and relationships that line bookstore shelves.

It is apparent that most all of us need help in our marriages. Most of us are simply too immature for too many of our early years of marriage to be able to deal with the inevitable problems on our own. I believe that formal marriage training should be required in order to get a marriage license. And if not required, then as a minimum it should be made readily available, strongly encouraged and voluntarily sought out.

There are excellent books on marriage, now, and far more is understood about how to amicably resolve issues that would otherwise damage a relationship. To not avail oneself of such help is, I am now firmly convinced, the equivalent of trying to fly without getting the proper training and a license. The risk is too great. As far as I can tell, there is no down side to seeking marriage training before the problems have created such a stressful atmosphere that reconciliation is all too often unattainable. To use the old farm cliché, why wait until the horse has run off before closing the barn door?

Colleen and I were lifelong students. We bought books on every topic that interested us and studied them at length, and that included marriage. As I have mentioned elsewhere, we found several books on marriage in our early years of marriage and studied them together. That helped us, obviously, but a lot more is known, now, about marriage and even better help is available. I would recommend any or all of the books that I have referred to in these pages. There are simply too many disadvantages to not doing so, and too many benefits from doing so.

I know there is still too much of the attitude toward mental illness, therapy and counseling—with all the negative perceptions of those terms—that existed when I got married to believe that our society will soon adopt a policy of mandatory marriage counseling, or training, prior to issuance of a license. I doubt that I would have reacted especially well to having to go to marriage "counseling" before we got married. Real men don't need no stinkin' counseling.

But Colleen and I are inveterate students. If a marriage "training class" had routinely been available, and had been a prerequisite to getting a marriage license, we both would have eagerly attended and thought it was a good idea—and probably both tried to get an "A" in the class.

So a lot of it is attitude and semantics. I accept that mandatory marriage counseling—oops, marriage training—is not likely to happen, at least in my lifetime. But I am encouraged to see how many marriage preparation classes are now being offered by churches and other organizations. I would encourage any couple that is truly serious about wanting to have a rich and rewarding marriage to seek out all the training and help available.

I mentioned before that my parents were excruciatingly private people. You simply did not, under any circumstance, air your dirty linen in public. That mentality was drilled into me from birth, and never completely left me. But I've come to accept that in being so private, you are destined to lead a rather isolated and lonely life. I've suspected for years that many of the men I knew as I was growing up ended their lives feeling withdrawn and lonely. Of course, none of them ever told me that, but there was a lot in their countenance that suggested it, especially in their final years.

I decided, at the beginning of writing this book, that sharing some of the insight that I've gained was worth what ever embarrassment it might cause me. I hope it may benefit others who feel the same as I have.

Now—on to lighter topics.

Chapter 13

The Best Medicine

By this point, you might be gaining an impression that making a marriage succeed over the long haul is pretty heavy duty stuff. And, in certain respects, that's true. That does not mean, however, that it can't be fun while you're at it. I suppose that a couple could have what they consider to be a successful marriage, and rarely find any fun in it, but that would not be my idea of one. Of all the elements that go into a successful relationship, and marriage, I believe that keeping a sense of humor about it all is probably as fundamentally important as any of the others I've mentioned.

Colleen was originally attracted to me, at least in part, because I seemed to always be joking and having fun. There's no doubt about it. I like to laugh and tell jokes. I especially enjoy satire and puns. As my kids became old enough to have to suffer and endure some of my bad puns, they began to dubbed "bad dad jokes." I was never clear on whether "bad" referred to "jokes," or to "dad," but the phrase has hung around for many years.

For most of us, it's not always easy to find the humor in life, or in marriage. It seems there is always something not so funny to have to contend with—although some couples do seem to get a free pass in life, skating along without much difficulty or trouble. There is a couple that Colleen and I have known for many years—I'll refer to them as "Bill and Suzy"—who seemed to never have any real problems.

Their life appeared to be a series of Ozzie and Harriet episodes. While the rest of us were having various forms of crap to deal with, they would have some little annoyance crop up, and then it would seem to miraculously work out and their life would continue on its pleasant way. It reached a point that it became a form of insider joke for Colleen and me. We would be discussing how it seems that we all have some difficulty to have to deal with, or some problem would be facing someone we knew, and we would observe, "Yeah, it seems like we all have our problems to deal with—except for Bill and Suzy, of course."

I don't know that Bill and Suzy would have agreed with our assessment of their lives. The problems they had to contend with may have loomed just as large to them as ours did to us. It didn't appear so, but trouble, like beauty, is usually in the eye of the beholder.

But that is not really my point. The real issue is not so much whether you will have to contend with problems in your marriage—there is a one hundred percent chance that you will—but how you deal with them, and with each other while you are dealing with them. And keeping a sense of humor during it all is the best possible antidote to trouble.

There are two kinds of problems, or trouble, that all marriages have to contend with, that I would call "external" and "internal" issues. There's nothing too profound about those categories, but they do have different sources and have to be dealt with differently. External problems confront us from the world around us, in our daily life. It may be anything from a disgruntled neighbor causing us trouble, to getting a pink slip at your place of employment. Those problems can, and should, bring us closer together as a couple. We close ranks and face the problems as a team. Oftentimes, dealing with such issues actually strengthens a marriage.

Internal problems are a different matter. Those are the contentious issues, both large and small, that develop between a couple. You don't like her spending habits. She doesn't like you wasting all your spare time playing golf instead of cleaning the gutters, like you promised three times you would do. Rather than bringing us together, bonding us, these problems can tear a couple apart and destroy a marriage, if not dealt with properly. And one of the best tools in finding a way to defuse such issues is to learn to keep a sense of humor where they are concerned.

Marriages have always had to deal with internal conflict. Two people can't spend a life together and not have differences. The iconic comedian, Henny Youngman, made a career of telling one-liner jokes that often were based on marriage, because he knew that everyone in his audience would be able to relate to the joke and see the humor in it:

"Take my wife... please!"
"We always hold hands. If I let go, she shops."
"My wife and I have the secret to making a marriage last. Two times a week, we go to a nice restaurant; a little wine, good food. She goes Tuesdays, I go Fridays."

Finding a way to laugh at yourselves, and your problems, is probably the hardest—and the best—thing you can do as a couple.

In *Why Marriages Succeed or Fail*, Dr. Gottman talks about how the couples he tested resolved their conflicts. Different couples had different ways, of course, depending on their personalities. He goes on to mention that the couples who seemed to have the best relationship were the ones who could begin to laugh at themselves during an argument or disagreement. He states that the argument might get rather heated, but then at some point one of them would begin to smile and within moments they would be laughing, and the anger would immediately dissipate.

That is not an easy thing to do. Even though I could see the humor in almost anything, and everything, I did and enjoyed making jokes about it all, I never found it easy to make funny during our various spats and fusses. I imagine that if I had been an uninvolved third party listening in, I would have found all sorts of things to poke fun at in our various disputes. But most of the time we were both too emotionally involved, and our egos were too invested in our own point of view, to see anything funny in the apparent unwillingness of our spouse to accept our position on whatever it might have been.

I am disappointed, looking back on it, at how we sometimes let some inane little issue boil up between us. A prime example, and one we've laughed about for years (later, but not at the time) was the infamous "cabbage caper." Colleen's diary reminded us of it:

February 20, 1957

Del and I had a run-in about cooked cabbage in vegetable soup, tonight. Seems silly, but was a point of contention between us.

I had the good fortune to marry a farm girl. Colleen was a good cook, and that served us well (literally) from the beginning of our marriage. One evening, just three weeks after our wedding, she made vegetable soup. As she had always done, and her mother had always done, she prepared cabbage to include in the soup. Problem was, I didn't like cooked cabbage. I most assuredly did not care for it being in the soup.

As Colleen said in her diary, it became a point of contention between us. And yes, it was silly. But those are the sorts of things that seem to happen to a couple. We had what turned out to be a rather heated dispute over the issue, and for a brief time had our collective noses out of joint.

We laugh about it now, and have for years, but we didn't laugh much about it that night. I won't tell you how it got resolved. You'll just have to wonder whether our vegetable soup has cabbage in it now, or not. It also makes you wonder how two intelligent people who love each other can let such an inane thing puff up so big, but that's what happens in a marriage too much of the time. That's why I say you need to work hard at developing a marital sense of humor. (I've wondered at times, since then: If the issue had been over having capers in the soup, would we have called the episode the "Caper caper?")

Another little event that we still use as an example of how things can work out—this time for the better—between a couple was the "keys locked in the car" episode. I didn't find the diary entry for it, but I'm sure it made it in there. It occurred more than ten years after the cabbage caper, after I had finished my Masters Degree and we had moved to Texas.

I got a call at work from Colleen one hot, Texas summer day. She was most upset at herself, nearly in tears. She had locked the car with the keys still in the ignition, and needed rescuing. She had the kids with her, of course, and because there was no such thing as cell phones, had been forced to trail them around the shopping center until she could find a phone to use. She was upset and embarrassed at herself, and further distraught over having to call me away from work to come unlock the car.

It took me about twenty minutes to get there. She and the kids were standing there, with nothing to do but wait in the hot parking lot, as I drove up. As soon as I got out, she started apologizing, and berating herself for pulling such a dumb stunt. I glanced in the car, and sure enough, there were her keys dangling from the ignition switch.

I looked at them a moment, then reached in through the open driver's window, pulled them out and handed them to her. She stared, speechless, at the keys now in her hand. It is hard to register absolute embarrassment and stunned disbelief simultaneously, but she managed to do so for a moment as she looked first at the keys, then at the open window. She had, by habit, looked for them in her purse, realized they weren't there, and had then seen them in the ignition. She was so upset about it that she hadn't noticed that she had left the car window rolled down when she locked the car.

There are times when you really do need to be kind, understanding and supportive of your wife—and that was one of those moments. It was also one of those moments when you want to laugh with your wife, and not at her. Fortunately for both of us, I was able to do those things, at least that time. I've always been rather proud of us for how we handled that one, especially considering how we mishandled things like the cabbage-in-the-soup set-to. I gave her a hug, assured her it hadn't caused a problem for me at work, played with the kids for a few minutes, and we went on our ways.

I imagine we had a fun time at the supper table that evening, joking about it. It has been a source of amusement for us for lo these many years, but it has also been an example for us of how much better we could both be about handling our problems when we could keep a sense of humor about them. I could have, in typical male fashion, vented some spleen about her dragging me away from work, for making such a dumb mistake, blah, blah, blah. I've been glad, as has Colleen, that I didn't do that. It was, in retrospect, a good experience for us.

There is one more of these little happenings that I want to include, as an example of how a couple can let little things escalate—and why you need to have a sense of humor about it. I was walking past our bookshelves, one day, and noticed a book I didn't recall we had. Its title was *Marriage to a Difficult Man*. That title didn't sit particularly well with me, and I was puzzled over why we had it. I pulled it off the shelf, found Colleen, and confronted her.

"What's the deal with this book? Did you feel you needed help dealing with your 'difficult man?'" I asked, rather indignantly. "Is there a companion *Marriage to a Difficult Woman*, that I can get?"

Colleen was obviously confused by my outburst. "I didn't buy that book. I would never have thought about needing it, in the first place. Besides, I wouldn't have been brave enough to bring it home."

That wasn't the reaction I expected. I looked at her rather blankly for a moment, then opened the book. Inside the cover, in my handwriting, was the message:

> To Colleen. Happy Birthday, from your "Difficult Man." - Del

The book, written by Elizabeth Dodd, was the story of the marriage of Jonathan Edwards and his wife, Sarah. It was from that book that I got the quote I use in the last chapter, where Edwards had referred to his marriage as their "uncommon union." It was in a letter of his to Sarah that he used the expression "dear companion," that I refer to elsewhere.

I—not Colleen—had purchased the book, years earlier, and had forgotten we had it. Edwards was a headstrong, but powerful and influential leader in his time. His towering intellect, unbending moral principles and "absent-minded professor" personality combined to make him a "difficult man" to live with. In spite of that, their marriage had been a long and fruitful one that was good for them both in a variety of ways. I had purchased it, somewhat tongue-in-cheek, as a birthday present for Colleen. I had wanted to let her know that I recognized that I, too, could be a difficult person to live with at times, but that she was my "dear companion," and that I felt that we, too, had an "uncommon union."

It took me a moment to morph from indignation, through puzzlement and, finally, to chagrin. Then, I could begin to laugh at myself and we had a good laugh about it, together. We've added it to our list of experiences to remind ourselves of the times when laughter should come first, and not last.

Our "points of contention," when we couldn't seem to laugh at ourselves, would too often not end until we had both said our piece, somewhat ad nauseum, and it became obvious that there wasn't much left to say. Colleen would then just decide it was over and get on with things, while I would all too often slide off into one of my "blue funks." But after a while, that would go away and we could then talk about it and come to some agreement and understanding on the subject. Then we could begin to laugh, and enjoy ourselves again.

Looking back at those times, I wish we had been better able to laugh at ourselves than we sometimes were, or at least to do so sooner than we did. We both have a good sense of humor. We often read jokes from magazines, or humorous stories from the newspaper, to each other. We find a lot to laugh at, and about, in our daily routine. I'm a little puzzled why we weren't able to make that happen better than we did when we were in an argument of some sort. But the fact remains, even if we sometimes couldn't— or at least didn't—do that, laughter is still the best medicine to cure an argument. That is, as long as both of you can see the humor in the situation.

The car-key event could very easily have turned ugly if Colleen had felt I was laughing at her about it. And Colleen could have become quite offended over my insinuations regarding the "difficult man" book. But as long as the one laughing can assure the other that it is the situation that is being laughed at, and not the other person, then it can quickly defuse the tension.

As I look back at my life and the people who have been a part of it, it is obvious that the ones I've enjoyed the most, the ones I liked best and wanted to be around, are the ones who found it easy to find something to laugh at—the ones who had a good sense of humor. I've read (actually, I've had it read to me—Colleen is always the one who reads the medical advice columns) that laughter releases endomorphins in our bodies, that enhance our moods. So there is, in fact, a literal truth to the old saw that "laughter is the best medicine."

Many things happen in life, and will happen to every married couple (except Bill and Suzy, of course) that are difficult and hard to deal with. They will not be laughing matters. They are usually not within our power to control. But how we choose to deal with them is within our power to control. Even though it may not be an easy thing to do, finding a way to laugh at those difficulties can help us find our way through them.

So my word of advice to any couple seeking to find the best in their marriage and relationship is to find ways to laugh with each other—certainly not at each other (although there are times when that is pretty hard to avoid)—and develop a marital sense of humor. Remember what Oscar Wilde said: "The man who says his wife can't take a joke, forgets that she took him."

There is always something to laugh at, if you look for it. My final word on the subject is to repeat a quote I found. It had no attribution, but I agree with it wholeheartedly:

"There are two secrets to a successful marriage: a sense of humor, and a short memory."

Chapter 14

Some Parting Thoughts

Writing this book has been a valuable experience for me. I hope reading it may in some way be just as valuable for you. Doing so caused me to think about my marriage, and marriage as a human experience, in ways I would never have done, otherwise. I have gained a whole new appreciation for what it truly means for two people to commit themselves to each other, and spend their lives together in a loving and supportive relationship.

There are two parts to that sentence that are fundamental, and too frequently devalued in our modern culture. The first is the word "commit." Colleen and I would not be enjoying the inexplicable bonding that we now feel, without the legal and personal commitments made to each other through marriage.

The second part is the phrase "spend their lives together." We are now experiencing a relationship, and feelings toward each other, that can only come from spending a lifetime together. Those feelings are of a nature as to now seem nearly mystical to me, and can't be explained—they have to be experienced. And spending your lives together is the only way to get that experience.

I have come to perceive marriage in much the same manner as when Dorothy started her journey on the yellow brick road to find the Emerald City of Oz. Standing before God and Man, and vowing to commit yourselves to each other in a legal marriage, opens the gate to a path that can be found in no other manner, that cannot be traveled alone, and that leads to a destination that exists only after a lifetime of traveling that path together.

I was not aware of any of this the day I got married. I only knew I wanted to spend my life with the girl standing before me at the altar of our church. You can see in the picture on the front cover of us coming down the church aisle, after our wedding was over, how I felt. I was holding onto her with both hands; I had her, and wasn't about to let go. We have now arrived at our marital Emerald City; we've found our Holy Grail of marriage. It is a reward beyond any I could have dreamed of, that day.

Although it has been a good experience, I can't say that I especially wanted to write this book. It's not that I don't like to write. Quite the contrary. Just not this sort of thing. But the old saw that "God works in mysterious ways" has hung around over the ages because the truth of the aphorism is constantly being revealed to us. As I said at the beginning—for the past several years I experienced first one thing and then another that ultimately led me to believe that I was being guided, maybe even compelled, to do so.

One of the more difficult challenges I faced was attempting to summarize, and organize, my thoughts. Life is sort of messy, and haphazard. It doesn't happen in an orderly, outlined fashion. You have to look through diaries and journals, sort through old letters and photographs. You have to ask yourself: Which ones of all those experiences were really meaningful, and had enough effect on me and my beliefs about my marriage, to make it worth including in a book? On the other hand, which ones were just… personal, and important only to us and only for that reason?

To help me avoid going off on some bunny trail on too many occasions, I turned to several books on marriage—some of which I've already mentioned—that I have come to respect. Some I had read in earlier years, but I also read several recently-published ones as I worked on the manuscript. I did so not only to help me organize my own thoughts, to help sort and sift fifty years of life into a few chapters, but also to see if my thoughts and opinions were in any way confirmed—or perhaps disputed—by the real experts in the field.

One in particular that gave me some pause in thinking about marriage, and my own marriage, was *The Proper Care & Feeding of Marriage,* by Dr. Laura Schlessinger. She begins her Preface with the following:

"Is there really ever such a thing as a *perfect* marriage? The answer to that question is, "YES.""

She has published numerous best-selling books on marriage, and has a popular talk-show. I figured she must know what she's talking about. But that claim took me by surprise. I was certainly skeptical, when I read it the first time. I've always believed Colleen and I have had a good marriage, but "perfect?" Frankly, it had never occurred to me that a marriage could be perfect. It seemed arrogant, maybe even delusional, to think such a thing. Certainly, I felt it would be hypocritical to claim it for my own marriage.

Dr. Laura, as she is often called, continues, explaining that "perfect" does not mean that everything goes right. She goes on to say:

> You can feel and believe that your marriage is perfect *if* you have the right attitude. . . . When you do so, marriage becomes perfect no matter what difficulties you're going through.

That contention caused me to do a lot of thinking about marriage, perhaps more than any other thing I have read.

I had a lot of trouble, at first, accepting or even understanding her point of view. It seemed too superficial, too full of pop-psychology. I felt as though she was merely capitulating to the "feel-good" mentality of our modern culture. I had trouble applying her rationale to my own marriage. To claim that a marriage is "perfect" would seem to require one to say there had never been a single problem; no arguments, no upset feelings, no bleak nights sleeping back-to-back on the far edges of the bed. My initial reaction was, "Balderdash. It isn't humanly possible."

Colleen and I disappointed each other at times, hurt each other sometimes. We had arguments, and upset each other. How could I be so presumptuous about our marriage as to claim that it was in any way "perfect?" But I kept thinking about Dr. Laura's explanation. I read, and re-read, her statement that, "You can feel and believe that your marriage is perfect *if* you have the right attitude." It finally began to make some sense to me.

On that Sunday in 1957, Colleen and I held each other's hands, looked each other in the eye, and pledged that we would each be loyal to the other. We pledged to love, honor, comfort and keep each other in health and in sickness, in prosperity and adversity, and to keep ourselves only to the other. We promised to love and cherish each other as long as we both shall live. I re-read those vows from our wedding service—several times, in fact—after reading Dr. Laura's claim. And then I began to understand it.

Nowhere in those vows did I find a promise to always agree. We did not vow to always be happy, to never have an argument or hurt each other's feelings. There were no promises to never be snippy or impatient. Indeed, everything in our marriage did not go right. We did not experience fifty years of bliss, untouched by difficulty, pain or trouble. But if "perfect" means that our marriage has been everything, and more, that we hoped for that day, if being true to the vows we in fact did make to each other makes a marriage perfect, then in that sense we have had a perfect marriage.

In spite of the problems we experienced, we have been true to our vows. We have loved and been loved, honored and been honored, comforted and been comforted in health and sickness, prosperity and adversity, all these fifty years. We have cherished each other, as we pledged we would do, and will continue to do so as long as we live. All that gave me a perspective on my own marriage, and what marriage is all about, that I had not thought about.

The problems, the conflicts, arguments and hurt feelings we all experience are not the issue. Being true to the vows we do make to each other is what makes marriage work, and makes it meaningful. Perfect or not, and contrary to all the negativity surrounding it nowadays, I am of the conviction that nothing else in life can be as rewarding, as beneficial to us, as a loving marriage.

To help bolster that conviction, I revisited *Marriage to a Difficult Man*, about the marriage of Jonathan Edwards and his wife, Sarah. I read it several years ago, but wanted to read it again. Edwards was a pre-Revolutionary War minister with an overpowering intellect, and was one of the most influential voices on religion in America at that time. He also served briefly as an early president of Princeton University, before his death in 1758.

I related in the chapter on humor the rather embarrassing story behind my having that book, so for present purposes let me just quote a passage from it. It is Edwards' last recorded words, made as he was dying:

> "Give my kindest love to my dear wife, and tell her that the uncommon union which has so long subsisted between us has been of such a nature as I trust is spiritual and therefore will continue forever."

That quote impressed me for several reasons. How can you not be impressed by anyone who could be that eloquent in their dying moments?

However, it was the phrase "uncommon union" that Edwards used to describe his marriage that especially appealed to me. I realize, now, that is how I have come to feel about my own marriage and what I believe marriage is meant to be. Marriage is an uncommon union, from several perspectives.

That perception was reinforced for me during a sermon given by the minister of the Presbyterian church where we are members, when he made reference to the book *Pensées* (thoughts), by Blaise Pascal, the seventeenth century scientist and philosopher. The minister was discussing the term "venerability," used by Pascal in his book.

By the term, the minister said Pascal meant "will it have a good effect on my life, will it make a difference for the better?" That question immediately struck a chord with me, and I made a quick note to refer to it in these pages. I realized that it sums up my attitude toward marriage. It should have a good effect on your life. It should make a difference for the better.

All that I've mentioned above is, at least in part, why I believe so strongly now that marriage is the best thing that you can do for yourself, why I feel so different about it than I did at first. When we were first going together, I was infatuated with Colleen. She was virtually all I could think about, all I was interested in. But there was no way I could have known in advance how our marriage would turn out. I didn't philosophize about it. I didn't wonder if it would work out well, or would be difficult. In truth, I gave that sort of thing no thought whatsoever. I just wanted to be with her and for us to share our lives. That meant I wanted to be married to her. I took it for granted that we would stay married.

Now that I can have a perspective on it all, I find that marriage was the best thing I could have done with my life. Colleen, and our marriage, had a good effect on my life. She made a difference for the better. She made me a better person. She gave purpose and a sense of direction to my life and made me want to do the right thing for her, and later for our family.

So in a sense, this book has been my soliloquy on marriage. Soliloquy is defined as a discourse by a person oblivious to any hearers present, often used as a device in a drama to disclose a person's innermost thoughts. I hope that there will, in fact, be "hearers" present, that some will read the book. Regardless, I've tried to disclose my innermost thoughts and beliefs on marriage.

If I were to be interviewed by a reporter about my marriage, I imagine his first question, even before asking me if I thought it had all been worth it, might be, "Mr. Hayes, you've been married fifty years, now. Do you have any regrets?" I would have to respond by quoting a line from one of my favorite Frank Sinatra songs, the poignant "My Way": "Regrets? I've had few. But then again, too few to mention."

In most respects, that summarizes my feelings about life, and my five decades of marriage. I do have a few regrets. Too few to be worth mentioning, probably, but I'll mention one, anyway. It is one which I suspect that most men, if they are honest with themselves, will admit they feel. Or they will, at some point in their life.

That regret is this: that I let the environment I grew up in, and my penchant for believing that "real men" were those stone-faced, non-communicative, undemonstrative men like Gary Cooper and John Wayne, make it virtually impossible for too many years for me to say to Colleen the things that I so deeply felt about her and our marriage. I have always attempted to let her know how much I care for her, never missing a birthday, Valentine's, an anniversary or the other special events in our lives. But it took far too long for me to finally be able to tell her in clear, unequivocal words, how deeply she had affected me all those years.

While preparing for this book, and for our fiftieth anniversary celebration, I spent a lot of time digging through all our memorabilia stuff. While doing so, I found all our pictures from when we were dating and first married. It triggered a lot of thoughts and feelings, and I've spent quite a bit of time talking with Colleen about them. She would tell me, each time I would make some revelation, that she always knew that I loved her—but that she had not comprehended just how deeply I felt it, or how much it had affected me.

I found it rather unsettling, and certainly disappointing, when she would say that. I had always believed that she was well aware of how nuts I was over her when we started dating, and got married. But I have to concede that I was strongly in the "actions speak louder than words" camp most of those years. So, even though my actions may have suggested how I felt, and I thought I was letting her know how I felt, I apparently did a far less than adequate job of doing so.

That attitude of never allowing your emotions to show, of never telling someone how you feel about them, permeated my entire extended family. I rarely found a picture of any of my relatives where a husband might have an arm around his wife, even casually, in the photo. I have seen plenty of them with the aunts and uncles lined up like a school class picture, all standing with arms at their sides, rigid as poster cut-outs. But I seldom found one with any touching going on.

Colleen and I did find one photo of my parents, taken when they were probably in their forties, or early fifties, where Mom and Dad are standing side-by-side. Dad has his arm around Mom's shoulder, grinning shyly at his risqué behavior. Mom looks stiff and uncomfortable in the picture, arms at her sides, as if she was embarrassed at being caught in such an unseemly circumstance. We could not avoid feeling sorry for them. But it pointedly reminded me of how much I had let that mentality affect my own marriage.

When Colleen and I were in a private situation, such as our home or the homes of our friends, I could be pretty relaxed about it. In most of our pictures, we look pretty cozy, together. That part never bothered me. It was when we were in public that my Kansas culture got the best of me.

I have an indelible memory of us from shortly after our daughter, our first child, was born. We had her in her little red and white candy-striped outfit, in her matching candy-striped stroller, walking the streets of downtown Columbus, Ohio. We were the picture of the idyllic young family. Colleen took my hand as we walked, but I withdrew it. I told her it made me uncomfortable to do that in public. I know it hurt her feelings. It created an awkward enough moment that I've never forgotten it.

It angers me now, when I think about it. How could such a thing possibly be the cause of embarrassment? I have a difficult time not being upset, in retrospect, at my parents and their uptight, repressed generation that fostered an attitude that it is somehow inappropriate for a man to hold hands with his wife in public, or to put your arm around your wife for a picture—or tell her how much you love her.

We are different people at age seventy than we are at age twenty. Life changes us. We see life differently after we've experienced more of it. And being married changed me. I now see my life in a different light. I was able to overcome a lot of those early inhibitions, as we matured. I came to be far more comfortable with our being more demonstrative in public, but it took me years to get to that point.

I guess I've somewhat redeemed myself in recent years. As I was preparing for our fiftieth anniversary event I found a CD with a piece of music I really liked, featuring a celestial harp. I created a video with pictures from our early years, and wrote lyrics to the music about how I felt about Colleen. As a surprise for Colleen during the anniversary celebration, I read a piece I had written about us, and how we met, then I had a lady from our church choir sing my song to Colleen. She was quite thrilled by it all, and I got a lot of good-natured ribbing from the other guys about setting too high a bar for them and their upcoming anniversaries. It all made quite an impression on Colleen. There is no way I could have done that in our earlier years.

So, yes, that is one regret that I have. I would like a chance to get to do that one over. I am "doing it over," now, in the sense that I'm not letting it continue for however many years we have left. It feels awfully good to do that, and makes me doubly regret the years I wasted by being too inhibited.

I suppose, if I let myself dwell on it, there would be other regrets I could mention. But I am reminded of the lines from John Greenleaf Whittier's poem, "Maud Muller":

"For of all sad words of tongue or pen / The saddest are these: "It might have been!""

As those well-known lines suggest, there is little purpose to be served in dwelling on what might have been, and I don't plan to do so here. I don't see how anyone can go through life and not regret some of the things that he did, or did not do. A regret we probably all have can be summarized by something Dad used to say, rather frequently: "Too soon old, too late smart." It sometimes seems to take us a long time to figure out what is truly important in life, and that inevitably leads to some regrets in our lives.

But enough of that. If some reporter did ask me whether staying married for fifty years was worth it, my answer would have to be, "Nothing else comes close." I presume from all I've said by now that such an answer would be obvious, but I'm not sure it really says why. I've tried to answer that, for myself, and find that it is very difficult to do so. Not because there aren't reasons, but because the reasons are so hard to describe in any straightforward way.

There are numerous obvious, but rather trite-sounding, reasons. I have enjoyed having a "dear companion" with me through thick and thin, joy and sorrow—fun times, and "spats." I like being able to laugh at ourselves, and some of the things we did, years and decades ago—or earlier in the day. Colleen once told a friend that we sleep "all tangled up." I like that, and stirring in the middle of the night, feeling her close to me.

I like having someone to talk to when I'm driving, having someone to call "Hi" to me from another room when I come into the house. I like leaning close to whisper one of my dumb comments during a movie, speech, sermon, whatever, and having her look at me and smile.

I like the comfort of knowing that I'm not alone, and having someone who can share my pleasure when things go well and comfort me when they don't, someone I can share thoughts and feelings with that I would not share with anyone else. There are more little reasons that I have liked being married for fifty years than I could try to list.

But those reasons don't really seem to get at the heart of it. There are also bigger, deeper reasons. I like having raised a family together, and now getting to enjoy them as adults, and to revel in the love of our grandchildren. I like the feeling it gives to look at photo albums and be reminded of all that we have experienced and accomplished together. But when, after fifty years of marriage, I sit and look at an old black-and-white photo of a curly-haired nineteen-year-old with radiant smile sitting on my lap, her arm around my neck, and have feelings so deep that it sometimes brings tears to my eyes, I have to wonder what is truly at the root of that.

I hope it was obvious from our "Sixteen Days" story how strongly I felt about Colleen from the very first night we went together. There's probably nothing unusual about that. I imagine that many, if not most, couples experience that in their own particular way. Perhaps it's just nostalgia, then, that causes me to react the way I sometimes do to those old pictures of us—but I don't believe that's it. I believe it has more to do with what I said about trust. I know that I didn't recognize this when we first got married, and probably didn't for many years, but when I asked Colleen to marry me I was asking her to trust me, to literally bet the rest of her life on me.

I recognize that a lot of the strongest emotions I feel now are those which come from being able to know that I did not let her down, that I proved worthy of the love and respect that she felt for me. I promised her, that January day in 1957, that I would be a faithful and loving husband, and I was true to that promise. I wanted nothing more than for her to never have to feel that the joy that was on her face in that old photo, and in our wedding pictures, was misplaced, or in the dark of some night feel she had made a mistake, that she regretted her choice. I can't imagine what I would feel now if I had betrayed that trust and let her down.

I now believe that a large part of the satisfaction of a lasting marriage is not just how you feel about your mate and your life together, but also how it lets you feel about yourself. I believe that I was a reasonably good parent, and that my three kids love and respect me. I feel good about that. I know my grandchildren love me. I feel good about that. I was a good pilot, with a perfect safety record over nearly forty years of flying Colleen and our family all over the country, in good weather and bad, and I feel good about that.

But I don't believe it is possible that anything could give me a deeper sense of self-worth, that would make me feel better about myself, than being able to know that from that first day, when I vowed to love and cherish her, I proved worthy of the love of that marvelous young girl who entrusted her love and her life to me—'til death do us part.

So there are lots of answers to the question of whether "sticking it out," whether getting married and staying married as long as you both shall live, is truly worth it. Some of those answers are simple, others are not. It truly saddens me now to read of all the young couples who have let our warped and misguided culture create for them such a negative view of marriage that they choose to opt out of it. I wish I could tell them what a good marriage can be, if they let it, and what they are going to miss in their lives if they choose not to create one.

But how do you describe a sunset to a person blind from birth? How do you describe Massenet's "Meditation" to someone who has never been able to hear? If I could do those things, perhaps I could then tell those young couples what will await them in a good marriage, what it feels like to journey through all your years with someone who becomes so much a part of you it is hard to know where you leave off and she begins. And perhaps they could then tell me what it is that that makes them so fearful, so doubting, that they cannot come to make that commitment to each other. Maybe I could then understand what has happened to marriage in our society. But I doubt it.

I will conclude with a story I read in *Guideposts* magazine. The story was "The Quest," by Ken Barnes. He had attempted to achieve his lifelong dream of sailing solo around the world, but found himself off Cape Horn clutching his EPIRB, a radio device that summoned rescue vessels, debating whether to push the button and end his dream. Severe storms had capsized his boat. His masts were gone, and he was at extreme risk of sinking.

As he hesitated, his finger on the button that would end his dream but probably save his life, he thought of his wife and family. He said he stared at the EPIRB, "as if God were giving me a way out, a way back to my family." Then he said a thought came to him: *Maybe my dream was about an entirely different journey. Maybe it was about the length one has to travel to truly appreciate love.*

That is my story. Marriage is that journey, that distance you have to travel together to come to truly appreciate love. I would have to tell those couples that fear it, that disdain it, that there is no other way to reach the "gold" at the end of life's rainbow— no other way to reach the end of your life with someone beside you who has loved you and stood by you, through every moment of every day, and who will continue to do so until that moment comes when you no longer get to be together. And then, perhaps, they could understand this: if there is a better way to spend life, and to end life, I cannot imagine what it could be.

About the Author

Del Hayes is a consulting engineer, working out of his home near Dallas, Texas. During his career he has published a number of technical articles. *Happily Ever After: A Tribute to Marriage from a Fifty-Year Veteran* is his first non-fiction work. His first published work of fiction, *The Old Man,* is a historical romance novel set in New England during the War of 1812. A second novel, *Ad Astra,* the story of a farm boy from Kansas who suddenly finds himself flying a B-17 bomber out of the jungles of New Guinea in World War II, is nearing completion. He has a second non-fiction book, *What Good Are Dads, Anyway?,* also nearing completion. Hayes and his wife, Colleen, celebrated their fiftieth wedding anniversary in 2007. They have three children and ten grandchildren (so far).

Ordering Information

Happily Ever After: A Tribute to Marriage From a Fifty-Year Veteran is available for purchase through Amazon.com, or directly from Homestead Press through homesteadpress.com. It is also available at select gift shops and bookstores. A partial list of locations stocking the book is available on our website.

Contact Homestead Press about quantity discounts for churches and other groups for use of the book in support of marriage training and preparation courses.

www.ingramcontent.com/pod-product-compliance
Lightning Source LLC
Chambersburg PA
CBHW051958090426

42741CB00008B/1453